Baseball
Is
Life
Is
Baseball
WINNING ON AND OFF THE FIELD

Charlie LaDuca

simply francis publishing company

North Carolina

Copyright © 2022 Charlie LaDuca. All Rights Reserved.

No part of this publication may be reproduced, stored in a retrieval system or transmitted, in any form or by any means-electronic, mechanical, photocopying, recording, or otherwise-without the prior written permission from the publisher, except for the inclusion of brief quotations in a review.

All brand, product, and place names used in this book that are trademarks or service marks, registered trademarks, or trade names are the exclusive intellectual property of their respective holders and are mentioned here as a matter of fair and nominative use. To avoid confusion, *simply francis publishing company* publishes books solely and is not affiliated with the holder of any mark mentioned in this book.

This book is non-fiction. However, some references to historical events, real people, or real places have been changed to protect for privacy as required by law.

Written permission has been granted and or attribution given for the use of all photographs in this book not taken by the author.

Library of Congress Control Number: 2022900201
ISBN: 978-1-63062-036-3 (paperback)
ISBN: 978-1-63062-037-0 (e-book)
Printed in the United States of America
Cover and Interior Design: Christy King Meares

For information about this title or to order books and/or electronic media, contact the publisher:

simply francis publishing company
P.O. Box 329, Wrightsville Beach, NC 28480
www.simplyfrancispublishing.com
simplyfrancispublishing@gmail.com

Dedication

To my father Sam who introduced me to the game of baseball and life. A hard-working truck driver, who always found the time to nurture my love of baseball while guiding me down the straight and narrow path of life. He modeled all a father should be, with a strong moral compass, and sense of humor that brightened our days.

I have fond memories of my dad coming home after a hard day's work, and never hesitating as I handed him his glove, asking if he would throw batting practice. We walked across the street, under the railway bridge to an open field. I stood at an imaginary plate as he threw our one and only baseball held together with electrician's tape. Time after time he would retrieve it and throw it again until I had enough.

If I close my eyes, I can still vividly recall the sights, sounds, and smells of old Offerman Stadium and later War Memorial Stadium in Buffalo, New York watching our home town Buffalo Bison's. It was the late 1950's and baseball was king in Buffalo. My dad would come home from work, fill a thermos with coffee while I grabbed my glove, and off we would go.

I anxiously waited at the ticket window as my dad got two tickets trying to avoid sitting behind one of the large poles that dotted the stands. Emerging from the tunnel as we entered the seating area, my senses were assaulted by the smell of popcorn and peanuts along with the strong odor of cigar smoke and a slightly fainter smell of stale beer. "Cold beer here, get your cold beer here," shouted a vendor. On the field were my boyhood

Dedication

heroes sporting white wool uniforms with their number on the right chest and *B* on the left. Sanitary socks and high stirrups topped off by a navy hat with the corresponding *B* boldly displayed.

Kerby Farrell led them to an 89-64 record that year. Good enough to win the International League Championship. Their names still swim though my head. Ruben Amaro, Pancho Herrera, Don Landrum, Dallas Green, Luke Easter, and my favorite Bobby Del Greco. I can't remember how many games my dad and I attended that year, but it was quite a few. The weekend doubleheaders were my favorite. As the light slowly faded from the sky, the less than adequate stadium lights illuminated the scene below with an eerie glow. A young boy and his dad sharing an afternoon at the ballpark. What could be better?

If you would like to get a flavor for my experience at the ballpark, War Memorial Stadium was where the baseball scenes from the movie *The Natural* were filmed in 1984 shortly before it was demolished in 1989. Watching the movie brought back all those memories once again.

I miss you every day dad and cannot wait until we meet again and have a catch.

Offerman Stadium Circa 1959
Photo courtesy of Bruce Orser

Young Charlie with boyhood hero Bobby Del Greco
Author family photo

Table of Contents

Dedication v
Foreword ix
Coaching Personality 1
Coaching for Character 7
Sportsmanship 18
Discipline 22
Communication 32
Team Building 39
Dress for Success 43
The Field 46
Goal Setting 49
Motivation 54
Play with Joy in Your Heart 59
Fear of Failure 63
Confidence 71
Umpires 78
Control What You Can Control 81
Postgame Learning 86
The Mental Side of the Game 89
Stephen McCoy 101
The New York State Championship 105
New York State Championship #2 126
Personal Wellness 135
Baseball Is Life Is Baseball 137
Sport Imitates Life 146
The Final Inning 148
Acknowledgements 159
References 161

Foreword

This book is centered around a magical high school baseball season that culminated in a New York State Championship. The preparation and lessons learned along the way opened my eyes to the secret of being successful, both on and off the field. Guaranteed success! No, not winning a State Championship every year, or a guarantee of landing that big promotion. This book outlines the secrets to *true* success.

It is not a book of fundamentals or new twists on old drills. Rather, it's a guide to unlocking the incredibly powerful tools available to you, allowing you to break through mediocrity and win the big prize. The concepts presented here apply not only to coaches and players, but to anyone traveling through this beautiful life. My hope is to impart a bit of wisdom and guidance as you grow to maturity in your quest to live a long happy life.

Like me, most coaches have attended clinics, read books, and watched countless videos of hundreds of coaches and ex-players teaching us the latest and greatest way to field, hit, pitch, catch and run the bases. I was always hungry for new ideas. Make no mistake, baseball is a very technical game. There is a wide variety of skills your players need to acquire if your team is to be successful.

This book is about the part of the game beyond the skills and drills. Every team in the country is teaching the same fundamentals in one form or another. Truth be told, the

Foreword

fundamentals of the game have not changed much in the last one hundred years.

Schools are classified by enrollment, meaning we are playing on a relatively level field at the high school level. What separates the best from the rest? Why is it that certain programs achieve excellence year after year? What do they know that others don't?

I have found some answers based on my thirty years of coaching at the high school level and sharing the field with professional players. My experiences are like most coaches. We win some and lose some. Players come and go as one season runs into the next. I was fortunate enough to build a solid program that experienced a great deal of success, if wins and losses are how you judge success.

We won our League Championship more than half of those thirty years, as well as numerous Sectional titles, Far West Regional titles, and (the big enchilada) two New York State Championships. It was the first State Championship experience that prompted me to write this book. It was an amazing ride - one that taught me more about winning and losing than all the previous years combined.

I struggled putting the chapters in a sequence that made sense to the reader. It occurred to me that explaining my philosophy of coaching, and how it influenced my first coaching program was a good place to start. Showing the results was the proper place to end.

Hopefully, my experience will help you and your team take the next step. This book will provide you with many tools to improve your program.

You will gain solid ideas to incorporate into your daily routine, taking your team, and hopefully your life to the next level. These skills have a direct correlation to success off the field as well, and in the end, isn't that what it is all about?

Many coaches are stuck in a rut, following the same routine, season after season, succeeding or failing based on the physical talent of their players. This book will give you an edge over your opponents. Most coaches do not have the luxury of choosing their team from fifty players who show up for tryouts. Most take who they get and make a team out of them. Rarely have I had enough players to make cuts. I am always looking for an edge, and believe I finally found it.

Even if you do not reach your goals in the win loss column, you will still have a successful season because you have taught your athletes, and perhaps yourself, valuable life skills. The character qualities and techniques I discuss will serve your athletes well as they leave your program and move on with their lives. A real win-win situation.

Coaching Personality

Above all else, we as coaches are human beings. Every one of us is a unique individual. Our thoughts, actions, attitudes, and appearance are unlike those of anyone else. When it comes to coaching athletes, our unique personality plays a huge role in the success or failure of our team. There is no perfect combination of traits or qualities that will guarantee success. No magic model all coaches can emulate. A successful coach with one group of athletes may fall totally flat with another.

What kind of coach was I? My core philosophy was an imitation of my high school coach Dick Myers. At six feet five inches, Coach Myers was an imposing figure. He was old school, teaching us the proper way to wear our uniforms, and the proper way to play the game. We respected him and played hard for him. One of his greatest qualities was his sense of humor and self-deprecation. He took the game seriously, but not so seriously that we were not allowed to have fun. I vividly remember he and our JV coach laughing so hard together during a scrimmage that one of them fell off the bench doubled up in laughter.

I was thirty-five-years-old when I began coaching. I was confident in my ability to lead, with a clear picture of the path my program would follow. In the beginning, my players were tough blue-collar farm kids. Strong and mature for their age. Self-motivating. They were extremely competitive, up for any challenge. An easy team to coach.

Over the years, the makeup of the team changed. The players were there for different reasons, needing several different strategies to motivate them. I am not one to lament the good old days, they were simply different, and I needed to adjust. My core philosophy remained the same, but I adapted my style of coaching to better motivate my players and make them successful.

I think, in part, I was able to do this because I was comfortable in my own skin, checking my ego at the door. My job was to mold these kids into players and good people. There was no room for my personal agenda. I approached it as a challenge. A problem that required solutions. The result was success on the field and based on my conversations with my players years later, success off the field.

Great coaches have a core philosophy that guides them; yet they can adjust parts of their coaching style as needed. Each season presents new challenges as players come and go. We often see this at the professional level. A coach is successful for a couple of years, suddenly falling out of favor as the losses pile up. Did he suddenly forget how to coach? More likely, he was not able to adapt his coaching style to the current group of athletes on his team.

Players join a team for a variety of reasons. Some are there to compete and excel, while others are there for the social value. You may even have a player or two who are there because their parents made them try out. Making your job even more difficult, is the varied range of skills within this group. How do you pull this group together toward a common goal? These are the constants I have learned: The players need affirmation, a sense of accomplishment, and (most importantly) they need to have fun.

One need look no farther than Lou Holtz as an example of a successful coach. His success is legendary. Over a thirty-four year coaching career, he compiled a 249-132-7 record. Perhaps he's most famously known for taking over the struggling Notre Dame Fighting Irish football team in 1986. The first thing he did was remove the players' names from the back of their jerseys to emphasize team over individual. It only took three years for the Fighting Irish to post an undefeated season and win a National Championship.

Coach Holtz accumulated many honors over the course of his career. He has been awarded numerous honorary degrees as well as inducted into several Halls of Fame. Perhaps his biggest honor was receiving the Presidential Medal of Freedom in 2020.

He has written or co-written ten books and continues to inspire with his motivational speaking, which is most important for the purposes of this chapter. What was the secret to his success? His players went the extra mile for him. They wanted him to be proud of them. If I had to break down his core philosophy as it related to understanding the needs of his players, it would come down to these three questions his players wanted to know about him: Can I trust you? Are you committed to excellence? Do you care about me? These questions must be answered with words and actions. Lip service alone will not cut it. The days of being the rigid "my way or the highway" coach are long gone.

Very few modern-day athletes respond well to that approach. The opposite end of the spectrum is the "good buddy" coach who wants everyone to like him. This may make everyone happy, but ultimately it's a recipe for disaster. Take a minute to analyze your coaching style.

Coaching styles typically fall into one of these three broad categories. The *authoritarian*, where the coach makes all the decisions without any input from his athletes. This style of coaching tends to limit the players' ability to think on their own and develop a sense of ownership in the program. Their personalities are squelched, and they robotically follow orders. Since the players do not have input, it can lead to rebellion against the coach.

Another style is the *casual coach*, who basically lays back and lets the players run the program. I see this style frequently used by young coaches. They tend to be more of a babysitter than a coach. A supervisor rather than a teacher. The players will typically enjoy this style of coaching. Everything is relaxed and fun. However, the greatest problem with this style is that the athletes will not show much improvement.

It is difficult to run a successful program if you do not take charge. Maybe you have a highly skilled mature team who can make this style work, but the odds are you will fail. Before long, discipline problems will arise, and things will spin out of control, leading to a messy situation.

The *co-operative coach* has the players sharing in the decision-making process. He has a plan and knows the direction he wants to take, and includes the players giving them some skin in the game. Players will work harder to achieve goals if they feel they have been a part of the decision-making process. It shows you care about your players and have interest in their thoughts. This style requires the coach to have confidence in himself and be comfortable in his ability to be in charge, yet know he may not have all the answers. It is a delicate balancing act. How much input from the players is just enough to achieve your goal of shared decision making without relinquishing control of your program? It takes a mature, confident coach to walk this tightrope.

The three coaching styles above are broad in nature. There is nothing that says you must be a pure disciple of one or the other. Most successful coaches use a combination of these styles to meet their goals. If you coach for any length of time, you will have many different players and teams. Each team will have its own personality. A great coach adapts to each team without forfeiting his core philosophy. A tweak here, and a change there, is what great coaches do.

If I were to examine a coach's style using an even broader definition, it would be athlete-oriented or win-oriented. An athlete-oriented coach makes the majority of decisions based on what is best for the athlete. A win-oriented coach makes his decisions based on winning at all costs.

The athlete-oriented coach will give his third string player an at bat or a spot in the field in a critical situation. It may cost him the game, but he has shown his player that he believes in him. What does it tell an athlete when you give him an at bat when the game is well in hand? Worse yet, when you pull him from right field in the middle of an inning because the game suddenly tightened up? Do you think your player doesn't know what is going on when you call time out and buzz him onto the basketball court with one minute to go and you are up by twenty-five points? Invariably, they are embarrassed.

I was a combination of the two. I felt a commitment to the competitive players on my team to win, yet also felt committed to taking care of my less talented players. This was made possible by the ability to play non-league games and scrimmages. They did not count towards playoff seedings, and as such, this was my opportunity to get everyone on the field. There were times I found a diamond in the rough who went on to make the starting lineup.

It was clear to all my players that everyone would have an equal chance to make the starting lineup when playoffs came around. I was going to put my best nine players out there for playoff games, but tryouts took place all season long.

Coaches are a bigger factor in the success or failure of their team than ever before. Twenty five or thirty years ago, young athletes were less dependent on a coach to perform at a high level. They were self-motivated, playing for pride and the team. Today, the coach must wear many hats to get the most out of his players. It takes time to establish yourself and to build a successful program. Hopefully, these ideas will help make life a little easier for you.

High School Team with Coach Dick Myers (far right) 1968. Charlie LaDuca bottom row fourth from left
Photo courtesy of Cardinal Ohara High school

Coaching for Character

John Wooden states the impact of coaching for character perfectly: "A good coach will make his athletes better players....A great coach will make them better people."

One definition of character is it is who you are when no one is looking. It is the "real" you. Your actions, not your words define who you are. Famous English author Os Guinness in his work *When No One Sees,* defines it as "the inner form that makes anyone or anything what it is. Clearly distinct from such concepts as personality, image, reputation, or celebrity. The essential 'stuff' a person is made of. The inner reality in which thoughts, speech, decisions, behavior, and relations are rooted. A person's character expresses most deeply what constitutes him or her as a unique individual."

The core of your athletic program *must* be coaching for character. If you do nothing else, you should develop a curriculum and *intentionally* coach for character. The laboratory that we call sport is one of the greatest opportunities to make a difference in the lives of young adults. I believe it is the greatest opportunity in your life to make a difference in society in general. A bold statement to be sure, but I believe it with all my heart.

I have lived it for the past thirty years, and the sense of satisfaction you can achieve is tremendous. Satisfaction in knowing that you have contributed and left your mark. I hope you have accepted the calling to coach with this in mind. If not, I hope to change your way of thinking.

The beauty of coaching for character is that it guarantees success. It takes the scoreboard out of the equation. If your barometer for success is the numbers on the scoreboard, you are setting yourself up for a rollercoaster ride of a coaching career. One that will often end in disappointment. Your job as a coach is to facilitate the growth of your athletes. Not only their physical, but also their growth as human beings and contributors to society. John Wooden was once asked about the influence he has had on his players. His answer was "ask me in ten years when I can see if they are good sons, husbands, and fathers."

The point is, one of the greatest coaches of all time understood his reason for coaching. He was there to touch as many lives as he could in a positive way. His goal was to use his experience and skills to mold his athletes into productive citizens. Every practice, game, team meeting, win, loss, bus ride, and rule had this goal in mind. It was a conscious effort to coach for character.

Many athletes in professional sports have set a bad example for young amateur athletes. They openly admit they did not sign on to be role models. Professional sports are a business designed to entertain and make money. For many professional athletes setting good examples for young people is not necessarily part of their agenda. There are numerous examples of high-profile athletes behaving in a way that should not be modeled.

What if every youth coach in the country made it a priority to coach for character? Not wins or personal gratification, but character. Eventually, professional sports might have a different look. What if young athletes at an early age who refused to buy into the good character piece were not allowed to play?

Participation in sport is a privilege, not a right. A pipe dream, maybe, but what if?

I made a conscious effort to coach for character shortly after I began coaching. That is when we started having a long run of success. Coincidence? I think not. It was easy to gauge our on-field success. We accumulated numerous league championships, regional championships, and two state championships. Gauging the off-field success of my athletes was a little more difficult.

I taught elementary physical education while coaching. My players were my students for seven years before they played for me. I knew them very well. I certainly cannot produce definitive empirical data that their experience playing for me made them better citizens. However, based on my observations both before and after they played for me, and numerous conversations I have had with my former athletes, I am confident that, in many cases, it made a difference. Like teaching, you will not reach everyone, but you will make a difference in some, and that is a worthwhile goal.

You will use the sport experience to teach practical life skills and positive character qualities. Your sport season offers a multitude of teachable moments. From the first day of practice to the last out of the season, situations will arise affording you, the coach, the opportunity to teach a life lesson. Just as every decision you or a player makes will impact the outcome of the game, decisions made off the field impact the outcome of your life. It is not a stretch to say that every decision you make either damages your character or develops it. Once you look at it in this light, you begin to realize how important it is for you as a coach to make a conscious effort to coach for character.

Reading this, you may think your job is solely to coach for character without regard for the success of your team in the win loss column. Nothing could be further from the truth. Coaching for character will pay big dividends on the field as well as off it. It is a means to an end. It worked for me, and I'm confident it will work for you.

If you have coached long enough, you have been frustrated by an athlete with excellent skills but questionable character. The player who has natural talent, yet never develops his full potential. Conversely, you have also seen the athlete who is an outstanding person yet lacks the skills to be successful. I have often thought how unfair it must seem to the unskilled player. He did all the right things yet could never perform like the natural yet undisciplined teammate.

The ideal combination of course, is a highly skilled player with outstanding character. This is sure to result in excellence. Skill without character leads to mediocrity; skill with character leads to excellence. Tryouts is a process of evaluating players with a goal of creating a roster for the season. All things considered, if two athletes appear to be equal in skill level, the one with character will be your most consistent performer.

Let me give you some practical information relating directly to your players. We can look at positive character qualities and tie them into our world as coaches. Players with character do not make excuses. They take responsibility for their actions. How many of your players are always making excuses? The umpire made a bad call, the sun was in my eyes, I had a fight with my girlfriend. Nothing is their fault.

Players with character do what is right rather than what is easiest. They run their sprints all out every time. They keep their grades up to remain eligible to play. When classmates apply peer pressure to break the rules, they walk away. Players with character do not take shortcuts. They have a moral compass and follow it.

Throughout the season, your players will face many challenges. The athlete with character does not quit when challenged. He or she accepts the challenge and perseveres. They will not quit after a string of bad at bats or failures on the mound. No other sport has as much failure as an everyday occurrence. Strong character is needed to overcome this adversity.

I have found that the words and actions of athletes without character do not always match. They talk a good game, but actions always speak louder than words. We have all coached players like this. The next time you come across this type of athlete, put it in the character box, and you will have better success understanding them.

Athletes with character rarely need external motivation. They are internally motivated to succeed and give their best effort. They value excellence and are willing to do what it takes to achieve it. I could give more examples, but you get the idea. Coaching for character is a win-win situation. Your athletes become better people which translates into success on the field as well.

If you are like me, you will immediately associate current players' names to this concept. This is a great tool to help you understand the makeup of your players and how coaching for character can lead to success on and off the field.

Here is a list of traits commonly associated with good character: Integrity, loyalty, honesty, respectfulness, responsibility, humility, compassion, fairness, authenticity, courageousness, generosity, perseverance, politeness, and kindness. It does not take much imagination to see how these traits would help your team to succeed on the field and your player to succeed in life. I passionately believe, all things being equal, the team with better character qualities will come out on top.

If you believe coaching for character is of value to you and your athletes, where do you begin?

I encourage you to read as many articles as you can about character education and coaching for character. There is a wealth of resources out there. Most importantly, you must model the behaviors you are trying to teach. One thing I have learned over the years is that your players watch every move you make. Your words and actions do not go unnoticed. Do as I say not as I do is not going to cut it.

I personally began my journey by implementing John Wooden's "Pyramid of Success." This was his secret to success, and mine as well. Back then, I read several articles on the concept, as well as his book. Now, he has a website: www.coachwooden.com. This resource is an absolute necessity if you are serious about coaching for character.

It occurs to me that younger readers may not know who John Wooden is. Those who have heard of him, may not know what a great and influential man he truly was. A small refresher course seems to be in order.

John Wooden coached the UCLA Bruins from 1948-1975. During his tenure, he posted a 620-147 win loss record, winning ten National Championships in twelve years, including seven in a row. He was named the NCAA College Basketball's Coach of the Year seven times, and in 2009 was honored by being named the

Sporting News "greatest coach of all time." His accolades and awards could fill this entire chapter. Perhaps one of his more notable awards was receiving the nation's highest civilian honor, the Presidential Medal of Freedom.

John Wooden the man, was more impressive than John Wooden the coach. His influence on hundreds of athletes is legendary. A long list of his former players went on to play in the NBA and coach at various levels. Most importantly, they passed on the life lessons this great man taught them.

The man, the myth, the legend passed away on June 4, 2010, of natural causes at the age of ninety-nine. His teachings live on in the form of numerous publications. A guide to playing sports and living life the way it was meant to be done is depicted in the Pyramid below.

Pyramid of Success

Image courtesy of Wooden estate and Luminary Group

The Pyramid of Success is made up of fifteen character qualities. Across the bottom of the pyramid are the following words: industriousness, friendship, loyalty, cooperation, and enthusiasm.

The next row contains the words self-control, alertness, initiative, and intentness. Above this row are the words condition, skill, and team spirit. Next is poise and confidence. The top row is one key concept - competitive greatness. I began introducing each character "brick" in the pyramid starting with one corner at the bottom of the pyramid and working my way up, presenting one word each week. I introduced it to my players at the beginning of the week defining the word and discussing what it meant and how it related to us as a team. The next step was to incorporate that word as much as possible into my practices that week. Here is an example. One of the words is *industriousness*. This is not a word you would normally use during a practice, but we all know it means hard work. John Wooden describes it as "the most conscientious, assiduous, and inspired type of work. A willingness to, an appetite for, hard work must be present for success. Without it you have nothing to build on."

At some point in the pre-season, we would practice baserunning using a drill that many coaches use. Place the players in a line behind home plate, and one at a time, they run a single and go to the end of the line. This is followed by a double, a triple, and a homerun. We were working on the proper route as well as always looking for the baseball as you rounded the bases. Invariably a player would not be putting forth his best effort. Many coaches would berate the player for "dogging it" or being "lazy." What if when you asked your player "why do you think I called you over?" he said, "Sorry coach, I was not being *industrious*?"

Let's take the word *loyalty*. Wooden describes this word in his pyramid of success in the following way: "Loyalty to and from those with whom you work is absolutely necessary for success. It means keeping your self-respect, knowing whom and what you have allegiance to. It means giving respect to those you work with. Respect helps produce loyalty." Here is one example of using the word loyalty in a baseball setting. Your team is on defense, and with runners on first and second base, you feel a bunt is in order. You signal your team that you want them to defend it using the wheel play. Your third baseman should charge and cover the bunt on his side of the diamond, while your shortstop hustles and covers third base.

The pitch is thrown, the batter slides his hand up the barrel of the bat and squares to bunt. Your third baseman charges home as the batter pulls the bat back and fakes a bunt. The shortstop fails to cover third base, and the runner on second alertly advances to third. A perfect teachable moment. Between innings you call your shortstop over and ask, "What happened out there?" The answer you are looking for is, "I wasn't *loyal* to my read coach." He failed to read the bunt and cover his base. Some coaches would rant and rave creating a scene saying things like "get your head in the game."

Or perhaps worse. What purpose does this serve? If you believe in the pyramid, you are intentionally coaching for character, and infusing words of character into your practices and games.

It should be noted, these words can and must be used in a positive manner as well. "Great job Joey, your *enthusiasm* was infectious today. Way to go." "Hey Jason, you showed a lot of *confidence* on the mound today. Great job."

Now I know this sounds corny. I thought so too, but I promise you it was one of the keys that won a state championship for us. To be completely honest, I felt a little silly in the beginning. Would the players buy into this, or laugh it off because it wasn't cool? I'm glad I discarded my fears and went for it.

Amateur athletes at all levels are exposed to the actions of professional athletes daily. Sadly, the lack of character and integrity exhibited by some has trickled down to all levels of competitions. There are certainly plenty of positive role models in the professional ranks, but those sending a negative message seem to get the most attention.

This trend will not turn around overnight. In fact, it seems like a very daunting task. Even overwhelming. How can one coach change the way athletes behave on and off the field across the country? Think about this. How many coaches today model themselves after their former coaches? I think we all reflect on the way we were coached, and incorporate bits and pieces of our experiences into our programs. We mimic the good, and hopefully toss out the bad. It is a given that a certain number of your athletes will go on to become coaches.

Let's say you are coaching for all the right reasons and setting a great example. If your athletes have bought into your system, and have a positive experience, it is reasonable to conclude that they will carry your teachings with them as they develop their programs. What if you coach for twenty years? Some of your athletes become coaches and some of their athletes become coaches and on and on. Not an overnight turn around, but over time, a wave of good character traits will sweep the country. In this scenario, what will sports look like in thirty years?

John Wooden - Great Coaches are Never Forgotten
Photo courtesy of Wooden estate and Luminary Group

Sportsmanship

Sportsmanship ties nicely into coaching for character. Certainly, if you are teaching life lessons as well as baseball lessons, your goal should be to teach your athletes to be good sports and all that goes with it. One of my proudest moments was receiving the league's sportsmanship award the year we won the State Championship. Not only were we recognized for our skill set, but also for the way we conducted ourselves on the field.

This was something I demanded from my players, as I felt we were representing our school and community. I had no desire to win championships with a bunch of players who were not respected. Winning with class was the only way to do it in my eyes. I drilled into my players that our opponents loved the game of baseball as we did. They enjoyed the competition and deserved to be treated with respect. Without our opponent, we could not have the ability to play the game we loved.

Once our program became successful, I found that our opponents and coaches appreciated our acts of sportsmanship. We competed in the Class D division. This was the lowest division based on enrollment and meant that there were times we played teams that simply could not match up. Like us, they were drawing from a very shallow pool of eligible players. It just so happened that many times our pool had more talent than theirs, which led to some lopsided scores.

Most years, I only had twelve or thirteen players on my team. When I was involved in a one-sided game, I would get my subs in early. Often it would not make a difference. I never asked my players to intentionally strike out, or purposely bunt back to the pitcher to make outs. It was a disservice to my players. More importantly, it made it obvious to our opponents that they were not a good team and needed help.

However, I would stop stealing bases, not advance from third on a wild pitch, and certainly not purposely run up the score. Coaches saw what we were doing and usually thanked me after the game. I would go as far as not report the correct score to the newspaper. What purpose does it serve to report a score of 33 - 1?

I frequently complimented our opponents during and after the game. If an opposing player made a nice play while I was coaching third base, I complimented him. Many times, I would meet the pitcher on his way to his dugout and give him a compliment accompanied by a fist bump or pat on the back. It came naturally to me. I love the game and appreciate a well-played game.

The result was a good relationship with coaches and players from around the league. When I run into coaches and players now that I am retired, we share a genuine friendship. We laugh and joke trading stories of the good old days. I never felt uncomfortable or the need to avoid someone because I was ashamed of my actions.

I don't want you to think that every coach and player along the way fits this mold. Naturally, there were a couple of coaches and players who got under our skin, trash talking and exhibiting poor sportsmanship. Generally, this was an isolated instance. We never lowered ourselves to their level. Our bats and gloves did all the talking. We maintained our poise, and just played a little harder.

Sportsmanship

After this pious lecture on sportsmanship, I must confess I broke my rule once, and only once. It was early in my career and we had one of the weakest teams I would ever coach. We played an away non-league game against an excellent team. At one point we were down 12-0. This coached poured it on. Stealing bases and scoring at every opportunity. I was boiling inside thinking about the embarrassment my players were feeling. These kids were my sport family, and they were being humiliated. That stuck with me for quite a while. It wasn't until three years later I was able to get my revenge. Just the sound of the word "revenge" makes me feel ashamed now. At the time, however, it seemed like the right thing to do.

Since it was three years after the beating they gave us, only one or two of my players were still on the team. Most of my current players were not part of the massacre. It just so happens, when our teams met again, we were loaded. We got off to an early lead, and I kept the pedal to the floor. I honestly don't remember the final score, but we beat them at least as badly as they had beaten us three years prior.

We lined up and shook hands at the end of the game. I had mixed feelings of satisfaction and remorse. Their coach gave me a wry smile. I had made my point. One I never tried to make again. I make no excuses. It was wrong, but sure felt good at the time. The proof I was not that kind of coach was that my players were surprised by my actions that day. I explained why I did what I did and apologized to them. The truth is, it cast a negative shadow on them as well.

In conclusion, teach your players sportsmanship. It makes every victory that much sweeter.

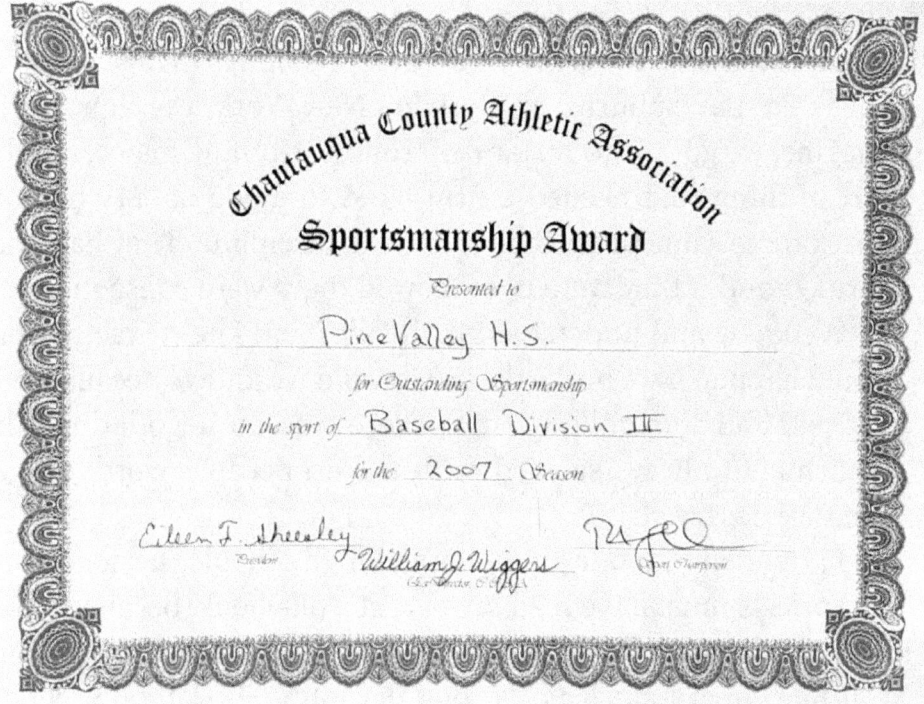

Sportsmanship Award State Championship Year 2007

Discipline

    I grew up in an era when discipline was a big part of family life. My mother was a stay-at-home mom, and my father drove a truck for a living. I was the oldest of four siblings living in a small house in the suburbs of Buffalo, New York. As you might imagine, we got into our share of trouble. Nothing major, but the sort of thing that needed a firm hand to guide us. My parents were on the same page when it came to discipline. They had a set of rules, and if they were not followed there were consequences.

    We knew and understood their rules and knew exactly what would happen if we broke them. How did we know? Because they told us, and they followed up. There was no negotiating. The punishment always seemed to fit the crime. In a word, we got what we deserved.

    I attended Catholic grammar and high school. The good nuns and priests must have read my parent's playbook, because it was more of the same when it came to discipline in school. I'm sure you have heard stories of strong discipline in Catholic schools back in the sixties. Standup comics make us laugh with jokes about the strictness of the priests and nuns. I am here to tell you it was no joke to us when we were in school.

    I'm going to tell you a true story that will seem unbelievable if placed in the context of schools today. The purpose is to illustrate the difference between discipline then and now, as well as parents' reaction to the discipline.

It was my junior year at a Catholic high school taught by Franciscan friars and nuns. Now we never saw the nuns, because the boys and girls were taught in separate wings of the schools. Yes, the boys on one side and the girls on the other. As one might imagine, this created quite a bit of tension as our young teenage bodies were filled with raging hormones.

I was in a math class that was taught by my football coach at the time. He was a lay teacher rather than a friar. Coach was late for class that day. What do twenty boys do when no adult is in the room? Of course, we were engaged in what was called horseplay back then. My best friend and I were in the back of the room standing up and playfighting, very innocently shadow boxing and laughing it up. Suddenly, the room grew deadly silent. I mean you could hear the clock ticking. My back was to the front of the room when suddenly my friend's eyes grew larger than I thought eyes could open. From behind me came a meaty hand that karate chopped my friend across the shoulder knocking him backward. I can still hear the thud it made and the scraping of the desk legs across the floor as he leaned back from the blow. Unbeknownst to us, one of the good friars in charge of discipline, heard the commotion and entered the classroom. We were the last two to realize how silent the room had become.

A feeling of dread washed over me. As I turned to see who had karate chopped my friend, I was whacked as well. The blow ricocheted off my shoulder and caught my lip. I felt the sting both physically and mentally. It was a shock to the system. I felt confused and embarrassed. Did this really happen to me? No words were spoken as the silent assassin left the room and we all sat down.

Discipline

About a minute later, coach walked in and sat down at his desk. Without looking up he said, "Hey LaDuca, how's your lip?" Obviously, Bruce Lee told my coach about the incident. My reply was, "It's been better coach."

I need to clarify that these were not full force adult blows. They were meant to send a message, not harm us. I happened to move in the wrong direction at the wrong time and caught a deflection of my shoulder.

The second half, and important part of the story was what happened when I got home that day. It was late, as I had after school practice and dinner had already been served. I went directly to my room. My Italian mother asked me from behind my door if I was ready to eat. I told her I had a lot of homework to do and wasn't hungry. To this day I don't know why she accepted my explanation, as I was a voracious eater, and she was an Italian mother.

I knew if she or my father saw my fat lip there would be other parts of my body hurting as well. Can you imagine this happening in 2020? I am confident there would be a lawsuit, and someone would lose their job.

I am not condoning physical discipline. I think it was and is extreme, but that is the way it was back then. We knew there were consequences for our actions and most adults were on the same page. I grew up with discipline.

I include the story in this chapter because it laid the foundation for my philosophy of discipline when it came to my style of coaching. No, I did not karate chop my players, but I did have a set of rules I expected every player to follow. They were clearly spelled out and applied equally to everyone on the team. Whether you were considered a star player, or third string utility guy, the rules, and consequences for breaking them were the same.

There are a couple of key points here - rules that everyone knew and understood, along with the consequences for breaking each rule. The rules and consequences were applied equally to all players. I have seen many coaches talk a good game, but when it came right down to it, they refused to discipline a star player when it mattered most. If Johnny was set to start on the mound the next day and broke a rule that should have benched him, he was let off the hook.

Typically, a way was found to delay the punishment so he could pitch the big game. Conversely, that same coach enforced the rules to the max when his third string player violated a rule. This was a show of false bravado designed to let the team know that the coach means business. What message does this send to the team? I promise you they all knew the reality of the situation. Different rules for different players. You just divided your team. This will simmer below the surface, finally coming back to bite you.

Many schools have an athletic pledge sheet. A set of rules that athletes must follow. Typically, a wide range of infractions and consequences are listed on the form, which must be signed by the athlete and his parents. I made certain we were all on the same page in our team meeting. These were the rules and consequences. They were not negotiable. I also had team rules. They were in writing, with a separate set of violations and consequences. Once again, everyone was made aware of them, and that they were not negotiable.

I took it personally when either of these sets of rules were broken by my athletes. They knew the rules and consequences

Discipline

yet chose to roll the dice hoping they would not get caught. They were jeopardizing the team's success because of their selfish motives. This is one reason I never bent the rules. The other reason of course was to build character.

I believe that the way I enforced my rules and applied them equally was one reason for our success. During one of my seasons, I was made aware of several players who had been drinking. At the time, it was a school and team rule that anyone caught drinking would be expelled from the team. Situations like this happen frequently throughout the course of a coaching career. My approach might be different than most. My initial reaction was anger. They knew the rules as well as the consequences yet chose to take a chance they would not be caught. Their selfish actions were letting their teammates and community down. How dare they!

We were having a good season going that year, and although some school officials knew of the infraction, they talked to the boys and hid it from me. When I found out, I called a team meeting and got to the bottom of the allegations. Three players admitted that they had been drinking. Two starters were guilty, including my number one pitcher and catcher. I calmly told them how disappointed I was and how they had let the team down. Then I threw them off the team. All three were great kids. I had taught them for seven years as their elementary physical education teacher. I had known their families for years. This was a tough decision; but I never wavered.

Years later, at a cool October home high school football game, I ran into the starting pitcher and told him I felt bad to that day about throwing him off the team. I felt genuine remorse, even though I know it was the right thing to do. He told me I was right to do it, and it was the best thing that happened to him. It forced him to re-evaluate his priorities and make a change. He had graduated from college, and was now a husband and father with a successful career. This was a moment I will never forget, one that reinforced my belief that tough love can make a positive difference in someone's life.

The follow up to that story is that the remaining players stepped up and we had a remarkably successful season. You need to be willing to make those tough calls. The sad truth today, in many instances, is winning supersedes life lessons. Many coaches will sacrifice a teachable moment to win a game. The trap is not being able to field a team if you are forced to throw kids off. I can honestly say I was willing to lose my season rather than give in to that pressure. There are many examples of coaches who have done the right thing and faced the consequences. They understood the magnitude of making the right and moral decision. They were developing character in their players. I tip my hat to them, as they are coaching for all the right reasons.

Early in my coaching career a veteran player broke a serious pledge sheet rule. Back then, the punishment was expulsion from the team. I discussed the incident with the player and told him that unfortunately he would no longer be a member of our team. I thought that was the end of it, but his parents put tremendous pressure on the school administrators to reinstate him. I certainly do not fault them for going to bat for their son. A parent's love for their child is powerful.

Keep in mind, we were a small school with strong family ties. Everyone knew each other, and had for quite some time. I had many interactions with the parents of this boy as his teacher and

Discipline

his coach. They were always supportive, making this decision difficult and uncomfortable. I knew it was the right thing to do; however, this did not make the decision an easy one. It was emotional for all parties involved.

The administrators gave in, informing me that the punishment would be four weeks rather than permanent expulsion. Once again, I understood the decision. This was a small rural school with strong family ties. I was not happy with this decision but complied. However, when the player had fulfilled his punishment and returned to the team, I kept him on the bench for two games.

It was my way of saying, your parents bailed you out, but we have team rules as well. After his two-game suspension he was back in the lineup, and being the adult in the room, I acted as if it never happened. I would like to think I saved some face yet made my point. Some will say you should have quit and walked away. Perhaps a valid point, but that would not be fair to the rest of the players. A cop out. I would suggest finishing the season and then resign if it is that important to you. Let a new coach start fresh.

I will end this chapter with an article from Full Gospel Business Training. I have been to many coaching clinics and although I did not see this presentation, I can imagine being there, front row, eyes glued.

A retired baseball coach was asked to speak to over 4,000 baseball coaches. The name of the coach who gave the speech was John Scolinos. He was 78-years-old at the time and was in the College Baseball Hall of Fame. He was the head baseball coach at Pepperdine University from 1946 to 1960 and at California State Polytechnic University Pomona from 1962 to 1991, compiling a career college baseball record of 1,070–954–13. Scolinos was also the head football coach at Pepperdine from 1955 to 1959, tallying a mark of 17–26–1. He also helped coach the 1984 Olympic Baseball team to victory.

When old coach Scolinos walked out on stage, he had an official baseball white home plate hanging around his neck. The audience began to roar with laughter as they thought this old man was some kind of comedy act their meeting planner had scheduled. However, the coach immediately asked, "Do we have any Little League coaches out there?" Several hands went up. "Do any of you know how wide home plate is in Little League?" Someone yelled out, "Seventeen inches?" "That's right," the old coach said. "Now, are there any High School baseball coaches in the room today?" Over a hundred hands shot up. "How wide is home plate in high school baseball?" "Seventeen inches," someone said. "You're right!" the coach said." "How about College baseball coaches, are you out there?" Half the room raised their hands. "Well, how wide is home plate in college baseball?" "Seventeen inches!" everyone yelled out in unison. "You're right," the coach responded.

Here is a hard question the coach asked. "Back in Babe Ruth's day, how wide was home plate?" Silence hit the room, then someone sheepishly yelled out, "Seventeen inches?" "That's right," said the coach. Now the coach changed his focus and asked, "What do you suppose a Major League team's management would do if a Big League pitcher couldn't throw a ball over a seventeen inch plate?" He paused; the room fell silent again. Finally, he said "They send him down to the minors or fire him!"

"But let me tell you what they would never ever do. They would never say, "Ah, that's alright buddy, if you can't throw a baseball over a seventeen inch target, we'll make it bigger for you - maybe we will

Discipline

widen it to nineteen or twenty inches so it will be easier for you; and if that's not enough we will make it twenty-five inches wide." Scolinos then asked the audience "Here is a question for each of you. What would you do if your best player consistently showed up late for practice? Or if your team rules forbid facial hair and some of your players started showing up on game days unshaven?

"What about if one of your players got caught drinking after hours the night before a game? Would you hold those players accountable, or would you widen home plate for them to fit their special needs?" The 4,000 coaches now sat quiet as the old coach's message began to mesmerize them. Coach Scolinos then turned the plate on his chest towards himself and took out a black magic marker to draw something on it. When he finished, he turned the plate around for the crowd to see. He had drawn a simple house complete with a front door and two windows. He then said, "The problem with most homes in America today - and with many organizations and associations - is that there are no standards for people to follow or people willing to enforce them.

"We no longer teach our children, our players, or our employees or our members accountability. It's so much easier for parents, managers, and executive directors to just simply widen the plate!" The result is that there are no consequences when people today fail to meet standards. Let's face it; we have lowered standards in education. Has widening the plate helped our schools? We've changed the standards in some religions. Has widening the plate helped our Churches? We have lowered the standards all across government. Has widening home plate made our governments better?" Then he turned the home plate on his chest around to reveal the backside of it again and said, "When we fail to hold ourselves, our children, our players or our employees accountable to any standards, our future gets dark." The backside was completely black.

Coach Scolinos died in 2009 at the age of 91. His message, however, lives on: If you're a parent, business owner, lead an organization, hold a public office, manage a department or supervise a unit of people, "Don't ever widen the plate" ... maintain and enforce the standards you have set.

The hardest part about being a coach or parent, is maintaining the rules or standards you have set for your team or your children. It is so easy to give in and bend them. Once you do, the reality is that you have no rules or standards. Kids catch on to this very quickly. There is an old saying, "If you give them an inch, they'll take a mile."

This is true of kids, who are looking for any loophole or weak spot in your policies and leadership. Consistent rules, consequences, and standards will benefit your athletes as people and, in turn, your team's ultimate success.

Bending the rules or ignoring infractions is the easy way out. It takes time and some uncomfortable moments to enforce all your rules. Please don't take the easy way out. You will regret it at some point.

Communication

Communication is one of the most important skills a coach can possess. It is much more critical when dealing with today's athletes than it was thirty years ago. There is so much to discuss regarding this area, I hardly know where to begin. I cannot emphasize enough how critical good communication is to the success of your team. It is not just limited to your players. Throughout the course of the season, you most likely communicate with parents, administrators, league officials, game officials, fellow coaches, medical personnel, and the media. It is the one constant that will take place in one form or another daily. Make it a priority to become good at it.

You will use many forms of communication throughout your season. We tend to think in terms of verbal and written communication, but equally important is non-verbal communication. You are constantly under a microscope. Whether you are aware of it or not, your body language and mannerisms are under constant scrutiny. Be aware of them and get them under control. One piece of advice I read and took to heart, was to have someone videotape you during a game. Have them focus the camera on you and you alone for the entire game. It is a real eye opener, and I encourage all of you to do it if you have the courage.

I would like to make some broad statements about communication before I delve into specifics. Communication needs to be honest, sincere, and consistent.

There should be thought behind it, coupled with facts or a philosophy to back up what you are saying. Try your best not to communicate in the heat of the moment if it is going to be negative. Allow everyone involved a little time to cool down. Communication is a two-way street. Listening is even more important than speaking. Strive to understand the other person's perspective. Allow your players to be part of the decision-making process. We tend to tell our players what to do. Create a habit of asking and discussing.

Communication is much easier for some than others. For me, it was an inherent strength that I was able to shape and improve over time, with conscious reflection and work. My advice to you is be honest and admit that you do not have all the answers. One of my secrets to success is being open to suggestions and not being afraid to admit when I am wrong.

We are human and have our strengths and weaknesses, as do our athletes. Showing your human frailties from time to time creates a bond with your players. Strong and confident, but willing to admit mistakes is a great base for communicating.

Communicating with your athletes:

My starting point with my players is always finding out why they are there. I have a one-on-one conversation with each athlete asking about their expectations for the season. What do they expect to get out of the experience? You have players on your team for many different reasons.

Winning is more important to some players than others. Some of your players aspire to play at a higher level, while others are there for social reasons. You must learn about each individual player thereby making the experience positive for you, the team, and the player.

Creating a successful program with communication at its core, will be difficult if you do not know where your players are coming from. Part of this conversation is letting them know my expectations for the season. This includes my expectations for the team as well as for the player as an individual. It is critical that you lay the groundwork for honest communication to flow in both directions throughout the season. They must know what you are thinking, and you must know what they are thinking.

I always strived to be totally honest with my players regarding their skills. Both offensively and defensively. They not only know what skills need improvement, but also exactly how to make that happen. They get the opportunity to improve these skills in practice sessions and games. I use non-league games or situations where we have a comfortable lead or a large deficit to provide playing time for them.

If they are sincere and working hard, I will never give up on them. My players all know that regardless of age, family background, or past performance, once the playoffs start, my best nine players will be on the field. The nine players who, in my mind, give us the best chance to win.

Communicating daily with your team helps them understand and accept your philosophy. Each one of my players knows his role on the team. Every one of them is made to feel important. Each player is an integral piece of the puzzle and will help us achieve our goals.

Daily communications with your athletes might be in a team meeting setting or one-on-one. Eye contact is critical. Scan each player in group settings to let every one of them know that they are important. In a one-on-one setting, make frequent eye contact throughout the conversation. There is nothing like eye contact to exude confidence while getting your point across. I cannot tell you what to say. It is your program. Speak your mind but remember to be honest and sincere. Most importantly, be a good listener. Your athletes want to know if you care about them as a person. I continually reflect on the words Lou Holtz passed on to his audiences during his motivational speeches across the country. "Can I trust you? Are you committed to excellence? Do you care about me?" These are the most important things athletes want to know about you.

I would like to think that I was able to make players want to play hard for me and please me. In part, it was because they knew I genuinely cared for them. The relationship between player and coach can make or break a team's success. These relationships are built on solid communication.

Communicating with parents:

There is an old joke; "Give me a team of orphans and I'll win a state championship every year." This is of course an exaggeration, but you get the point. One of the primary reasons that veteran coaches at the youth or high school level resign or retire, is their lack of desire to deal with parents. The mothers and fathers of your players can be a blessing or a curse. I certainly do not want to paint them all with the same brush. It is natural for a parent to overestimate the skills of their child. Honestly, it would be a little odd if they didn't. Often, however, the parents of your players become a disruptive force in your program.

You have a philosophy. One that has been endorsed by whomever hired you for the job. Your philosophy may be at odds with certain parents, but ultimately you are the coach, and you must be true to yourself. I am not saying we as coaches are always right, but right or wrong, it is our program to run until someone in authority tells us it is not. Parents are as much a part of your season as your opponents, umpires, and the weather.

Rather than fight them and let them get the best of you, learn how to deal with them. As is true with your players, communication is vitally important. Equally important, however, is having a thick skin.

You are going to hear things directly or through the grapevine that will not be very complimentary. Be the adult in the room, have confidence in your philosophy, and move on.

I strongly recommend a pre-season meeting with your parents and players. Lay out your philosophy and expectations in clear terms. Talk about your rules, discipline, playing time, and anything you can think of that might be a concern. Remember what you said and do not waiver from it as the season progresses. You must have an open-door policy, one that truly makes the parents feel they can contact you and openly discuss their concerns. Let them know the best time and method to contact you. I made it a policy to not entertain concerns or problems directly before, during, or after a game.

This was my time to focus on the task at hand. Any other time was fine with me. The general rules of communication as stated above apply. I can assure you that I have had many such conversations over the years. I cannot say they all ended with the parent's satisfaction and being in total agreement with me, but I always followed my rules of communication. I tried my best to make them understand my point of view and to understand theirs.

Communicating with the media:

This is a skill that must be developed. Positive press will go a long way toward promoting your program and boosting the morale of your players and community.

Sports reporters are looking for a good story. They want to know the inside scoop. What happened and why? What were you thinking at that moment? Tell me about that call? They have a job to do. Help them do their job.

It came easily to me, but I know this is not the case for many coaches. I never brushed off a reporter. Win or lose, I gave them a story. I was honest, did not make excuses and never, and I mean never, threw anyone under the bus. My comments were humble and complimentary to our opponent. I would tell them anything they wanted to know for as long as it took. Invariably, I injected a little humor, as this was just my style.

The result was a great relationship with the media. We received more press than any team in the county. Granted, we were successful, but they always had a great deal of quotes and material to work with, making their job easier. A bonus was how much my players loved seeing their name and picture in the paper.

I fondly remember one of my players sprinting from the parking lot to our field as practice was about to begin. He was waving the morning paper and shouting, "Hey, did you guys see this?" It was a story on the front page of the sports section with him dealing from the mound. Priceless.

Communication

Mound meeting Fredonia Baseball Team 2018
Photo courtesy of The Post-Journal

Addressing Media Post NYS Championship 2007
Scott Kindberg Jamestown Post Journal
Photo courtesy of The Post-Journal

Team Building

Two of the most important factors in taking your team to the next level, are the mental part of the game, and the bond within your group of players. I sit down at the end of each season and judge my failure or success on a simple concept. In my opinion, based on the players we had, did we overachieve or underachieve? As simple as that. It is difficult to control the scoreboard; and if that is your barometer of success or failure, you are setting yourself up for failure. Bad bounces, bad calls, weather, and injuries are all, for the most part, out of your control. What is in your control, is assessing the skill and needs of your players and using that information to make them the best they can be.

Overachieving can be very elusive. In my experience, a group of players who come together as one, have an excellent chance of meeting that goal. Your team will be made up of players who have a wide variety of interests and personalities. They are not all there for the same reason. The first step is communicating with them to find out what each one of them expects to get out of the season. Once you have a handle on where they are coming from, you need to make a conscious effort to get them all on the same page.

For us, the ultimate goal, if we are talking about wins and losses, is to win the championship game.

Naturally, you will have smaller goals along the way leading up to that point. You are all in this together. Everyone must focus on the goal, and together it can be achieved. There are so many

Team Building

distractions along the way that it is hard to put them all into writing. During a season, parties, vacations, alcohol, drugs, personal relationships, and jobs are all potential distractions. How in the world can you get all these things off the table so your players can focus on your goals?

It is important that each player feels a part of the team with a role to play. You need everyone to make it happen, no matter how big or small their role may be. One team, one family. They need to hang out together and be supportive. They must cheer each other on rather than hoping someone will fail so they get their chance to play. This is a hard concept for young players. And an especially hard concept for their parents. Make them all feel important.

I had many talks with my teams about the hazards of outside influences and how important it was to hang out with the right crowd. *You are the company you keep.* It has been my experience that many so-called friends take pleasure in bringing the athlete down and showing everyone that the hot shot ballplayer is no better than they are. I have seen this time and time again.

The Senior Trip is a tradition held by many high schools. Our trip took place every year toward the end of our baseball season. The trips started out as educational trips to Gettysburg or Washington, D.C. They evolved into trips to Disney World and other less educational destinations. It is always a nerve wracking time for spring sport coaches. Chaperones went along, but there was plenty of time for kids to get into trouble if they were so inclined.

Typically, there was a little free time built in for the kids to go exploring on their own. Unfortunately, a group ended up at a

Hooters for lunch. Naturally, pictures were taken of this major coup during a Senior Trip. This was before social media was a thing; however, hard copies of the pictures began circulating once the kids returned home. Somehow, they made their way to our school administrators. Two of my ball players happened to be prominently displayed front and center with beers in hand. Based on my knowledge of who was there, I am confident it was a set up to bring two well-liked popular athletes down a peg. Naturally, they were disciplined and removed from the team. Not the friends I want in my life.

I tried to educate my players on the dangers of attending these parties. Everything they do is now out in the open due to the far reach of social media.

My answer to this reality was to encourage my players to remain a team off the field. Hang out together. Have their own social events and police themselves. The hope is that you have instilled the importance of the pledge sheet they have signed.

The pledge sheet is a formal document that you as a coach, and they as players must take seriously. Emphasize team. Emphasize family. Hammer on it every day. Create pride in who they are and what they represent. Younger kids in school look up to them. They represent the school and community. Make them feel special. Have pizza parties, and fun events that have nothing to do with baseball. When conflicts arise between players, address them quickly. Talk it out. There will be a hundred teachable moments during the season. Do not let one pass by without taking advantage of it.

It is always devastating when a player breaks the rules and is thrown off the team. Honestly, getting your entire team on the same page is incredibly difficult. Give it your best shot. You are building a program. Slowly but surely, over time, you will achieve your goal.

Like most chapters in this book, there are lessons that carry over to everyday life. Make a conscious effort to surround yourself with positive people. Friends who want what is best for you rather than those who may be jealous and want to tear you down. Avoid negative people. Surround yourself with friends who have the same goals. Life, like sport, has many ups and downs. It is difficult to navigate alone. If you think about it, like a sports team, we hold tryouts. People come into our lives hoping to join our "team." Choose carefully.

Dress for Success

One of the main challenges a coach faces trying to take his team to the next level, is building a sense of pride in his players. Many of my players over the years came from lower income families trying to make ends meet. Often, they were judged based on where they lived or what kind of clothes they wore. My goal was to give these players a chance to be a part of something special. A chance for younger kids, peers, and adults in the community to look at them with respect and admiration. I have voiced many times that I did not care what part of the tracks they came from, or what their last name was. When they put on our uniform, they became part of a special family.

It is said that you never get a second chance to make a good first impression. I am here to tell you, it does make a difference. We wore our uniforms with pride. Hats on straight, shirts tucked in, gig line straight, (a military term referring to buttons, belt buckle, and zipper in a straight line), shoelaces tied, and clean spikes. We looked that way before the game, after the game, at our food stop, and on the bus ride home. Our school was in a rural community. Most homes had well water, which made it hard to keep our uniforms bright. I collected all the uniforms and laundered them myself (with the help of my wife) after every game. It was a little extra work and went a long way toward creating that feeling of being a part of something special. It was one more way to build pride and confidence.

Dress for Success

There were times when our bus would pull up to a field while our opponent was going through their pre-game warm-up. My kids would take one look at the way they were sloppily dressed and comment on it. I would ask, "Who do you think will win today?" Most of the time we did. Usually it was because we were a better team, but part of what made us a better team was our sense of pride. We took pride in our appearance, in our actions, and in winning.

We pulled into a fast-food parking lot after a game one day. As the players were getting off the bus, a rookie walked down the aisle with his shirt untucked. A veteran asked him where he was going. "I'm going to eat," he replied." "Not until you tuck your shirt in," said the veteran player. That was a proud moment for me indeed.

I was a stickler about appearance. If a player forgot part of his uniform, he did not play that day. If his shirt tail popped out during a game, we called time out and he tucked it in. I carried cleaning supplies for spikes with me on the bus. It was just a way of life. Once it was established, the players themselves passed it along to the new members of the team.

During practice, we wore gray baseball pants, a purple shirt, and our team hat. If it was exceptionally hot, we wore gray or black shorts and a purple shirt. We were a team. This may sound trivial, but it was one of our foundations for success. Remember, these are tips designed to take you to the next level. Do not sell them short.

I felt walking off the bus as a team, looking sharp and portraying confidence was worth two runs before we even took the field. Our opponents took notice and knew we were serious about the game at hand. We have been taught not to judge people by the way they look, and I think that is sound advice, but in many instances, it's quite a difficult task.

One of the jobs I had before I began my teaching career involved hiring employees. I must admit, a candidate who entered my office looking as if they took pride in their appearance made an immediate impression. This told me they were serious about getting the job. The quality of the clothing was not important. Like some of my players, not everyone has access to expensive clothing. What was important was the effort it took to look good and professional.

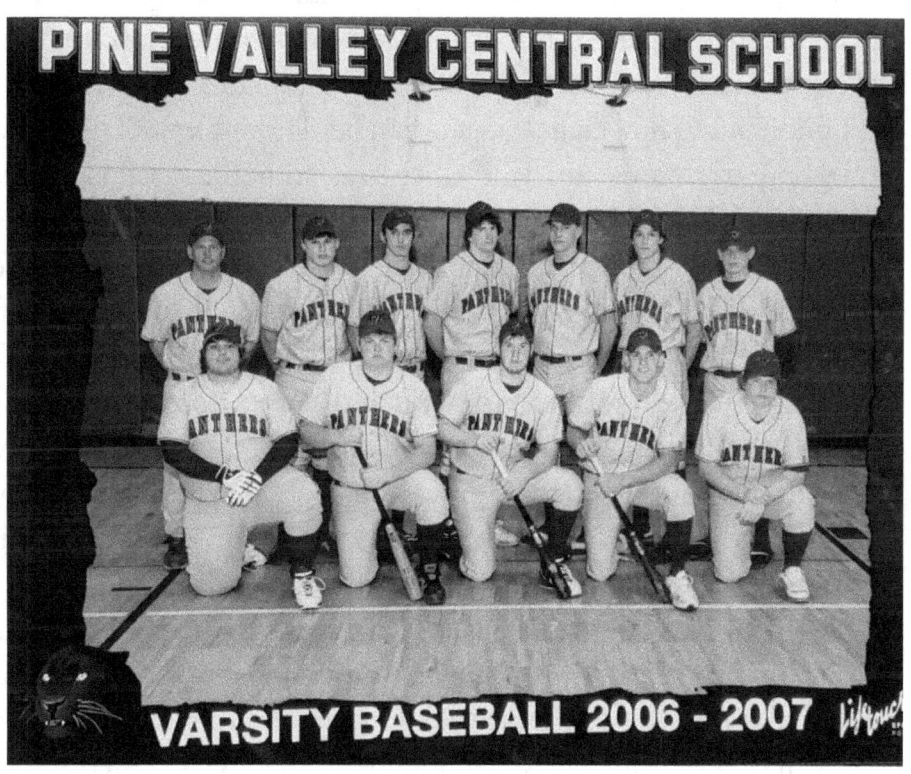

NYS Championship Team Pre-Season Picture Dressed for Success
Photo courtesy of Pine Valley Central School

The Field

Your baseball field is a big part of your failure or success. The condition of your playing surface impacts many parts of the game. Bad bounces, pitchers struggling with the mound, batters uncomfortable in the batter's box, holes in the outfield, and high uncut grass are just a few of the things that can alter the course of a game. More importantly, there is a safety factor to consider. However, it goes beyond that. If you buy into the concept that pride and confidence will help your team advance to the next level, a nice-looking ball field is one of the most important places to start.

I understand how tight budgets can be. The amount of time and money organizations are willing to put into their fields varies significantly. I was fortunate enough to have a maintenance crew that took tremendous pride in our field. In the early days, I cut the grass, dragged the field, and lined it, doing most of the work myself. Slowly but surely the maintenance crew became more involved. Eventually, they threw me off the field and told me to get out of their way. Whether it is a youth league, high school or college, there are simple things you can do to improve your field. I believe that one of the most important things you can do is to show everyone that you are willing to roll up your sleeves and get your hands dirty.

It is important that your players take pride and get involved as well. Set up a rotating schedule of field maintenance to be performed by your players. On off days, we would spend a couple of hours as a team working on the field. After a game, a sheet was posted in the dugout of every player's duties. Raking, filling holes, tarping the mound and home plate, were just some of the assigned duties. It went quickly, and never let our field get beyond the point of repair. Opposing teams loved coming to our field.

My greatest moment of pride was when a group of players petitioned the school board to name the field after me. Now everyone who plays on that field sees my name prominently displayed above the scoreboard.

My meticulousness regarding the ball field came from my upbringing. I grew up in a small house with an even smaller yard. My father took pride in the house and yard. He maintained the lawn and flower beds on a weekly and sometimes daily basis. I do the same with my property. Home life and baseball life once again intertwined.

Take ownership in the condition of your field. Here are a couple of sites to get you started. There are numerous articles and books and websites at your fingertips.

Basic Baseball field Maintenance
https://sportsfieldmanagementonline.com/2016/04/19/basic-baseball-field-maintenance/7955/

Managing and Repairing Lips on Baseball Fields
https://sportsfieldmanagementonline.com/2015/03/10/managing-repairing-lips-on-baseball-softball-fields/6853/

Maintenance Tips: What You Can Do to Improve the Playability, Durability of Your Little league Field
https://www.littleleague.org/university/articles/field-maintenance-tips-what-you-can-do-to-improve-the-playability-durability-of-your-little-league-field/

The Field

Charlie LaDuca Field. Pine Valley Central School

Goal Setting

Goal setting is a tricky business. It is important to set reachable yet challenging goals that progress throughout a season. Knowing your athletes is critical when it comes to setting goals, as you will set individual as well as team goals. Once you set your goals, you better have a plan to achieve them.

Setting specific goals increases motivation, accountability, focus, and productivity. There has been much research on the results when setting goals in business settings, academic settings, and athletic settings. Peter Drucker's Management by Objectives concept discusses SMART goals. An acronym for: Specific, Measurable, Attainable, Realistic, and Timed. "Goals should be concrete and measurable – would any outside observer be able to tell whether the goal has been met or not? Ensure that goals are challenging, but realistic. Goals should be challenging enough to encourage growth, but achievable enough that success can eventually be met. When athletes create and achieve goals, it creates a winning mindset."

Studies show that simply writing down goals can increase the likelihood that those goals will be achieved. Within the framework of a team, it is important for each player to set individual goals and for the team to set group goals. Each player should recognize how their goal is tied to the collective team goal. When they realize the importance of their contribution to the team, they will be more open to feedback and making improvements. Monitoring progress towards smaller goals

Goal Setting

encourages athletes to constantly improve and to build new habits.

When choosing individual goals for your players, be sure to refer to your one-on-one conversations. What is important to this athlete? What is possible for them to achieve? As a coach, try not to dictate the individual goals, instead serve as a facilitator, helping the athlete to recognize strengths and possibilities, as well as how they can contribute to the team goal. When players are involved in creating and monitoring their own goals, this ownership will create a greater sense of pride in achieving them.

Goals provide a concrete representation of the hopes and dreams to which the player feels committed. This investment and internal motivation become a key element in self-control and the ultimate "mind over matter" goal: building players' ability to self-monitor, control, and change their own thoughts and actions. Having a personal goal forces the athlete to be aware of and accountable for every action that they take. This accountability further reinforces the premise that they are responsible for their own actions and that these actions contribute largely to both individual and team success, regardless of any obstacles that may be encountered.

As a coach, it is your job to assist players in monitoring their goals and to provide specific feedback towards corrective actions. This will be crucial in helping the athlete to adjust accordingly so that goals can be achieved. Additionally, teammates can also be essential in providing feedback and holding one another accountable in achieving their goals. There is immense power in peer pressure, as players often value the opinions of their teammates more than that of anyone else.

Baseball Is Life Is Baseball

As imperative as it is to set and monitor goals, it is equally important to celebrate the achievement of goals, both big and small. This allows the opportunity for team members to support one another and to celebrate success together, which contributes to team bonding, cooperation, and the feeling of family. You don't have to win every game. You don't have to give everyone a participation trophy. You do have to recognize each player when they are working hard and meeting individual and team goals. Everyone needs to feel like an integral part of the system, a crucial cog in the machine.

I had a player on my team who was a notorious pull hitter. If he got an inside pitch, he rarely missed it, hitting the ball hard to the left side of the field. It did not take long for opposing pitchers to throw him a steady diet of curve balls, changeups, and fastballs away. As his batting average fell, his frustration rose. I was forced to move him down in the lineup, and eventually out of it entirely. He had become an automatic out.

Being a competitor, he was willing to make some changes. We set a goal of hitting outside pitches to the right side of the field. I failed to mention that he was a right-handed batter. This meant letting the ball travel deeper into the hitting zone and creating an inside-out approach to the ball. This not only required different timing on his part, but also a mechanical adjustment to the path of his swing.

I find this to be one of the most difficult things to teach a hitter. It takes repetition and a strong will to succeed. We began working in the off season, drill after drill, repetition after repetition. When our season officially began with practices in the gym, he had made significant progress in achieving his goal. The reward for his hard work was not long in coming. In our second

Goal Setting

game of the season, he hit a walk off single to right field to win the game. In our team meeting on the field after the game, I heaped praise on him telling the team how hard he worked in the off season. Naturally, he was beaming, and an example had been set for the rest of the team.

Baseball, more than any sport, is statistically driven. Major League Baseball publishes eighty-five different stats. Twenty-eight batting stats, forty-two pitching stats, and fifteen fielding stats. Somewhere within these stats, is an opportunity to set individual and team goals.

Individual hitting goals can include limiting strikeouts in a season. It can be a specific number. "My goal is to strike out less than ten times this year." The player may set a specific batting average or number of stolen bases as a goal. Pitchers might set a goal of limiting walks per game. A fielder could set a goal of limiting errors or increasing his fielding percentage. Any stat can be set as a goal.

Goals, however, are not limited to stats. "I will have better body language this season". "I will run hard every time I hit the ball." "I will be a better teammate." "I will maintain my grades so I remain eligible to play."

Team goals can be agreed upon as a collective group. They usually start small, and end where the team thinks they can reasonably finish.

The years we had a strong team, one of our goals was to win a state championship. Our goals leading up to that were to win our league, section, and far west regional game sending us to the state final four. There were years our goal was to finish above five hundred in league play. Remember, the goals must be realistic and attainable.

In conclusion, goal setting is an integral part of success. The fun part is defining the specific drills and skills needed to achieve your goals. Breaking down practice sessions with a short-term goal allows you and your team to achieve your long-term goals. This is coaching at its best.

Motivation

When it comes to motivation, I think the job of the coach is much harder today than it was several years ago. There seem to be fewer and fewer self-motivated athletes. Motivation is a big part of your purpose as a coach. Complicating matters is that many of your athletes need to be motivated in different ways. A technique that might light a fire under one athlete, may totally turn off another. That is why it is so important to get to know your athletes individually. Why are they there? What do they expect to get out of the season? These are questions that must be answered if you have any hope of being successful. The only way to get these questions answered is to sit down with each of your players individually and ask them those two questions: "Why are you here?" and "What do you expect to get out of the season?"

I do a little exercise with my players at the start of the season that works nicely. I give each player a blank piece of paper asking them to write the headline and a newspaper article as if our season had just ended. What would it say? What was the major headline, and what was the story? I encourage them to write both a personal and a team headline and story. How would they like the season to end in specific terms? It really opens your eyes to the expectations of your players.

I found the motivational piece to be the most exciting part of the job. Anybody can hold a practice or physically coach a game. It takes a good coach to motivate a team to seek athletic greatness. Assessing the needs of each player and meeting those needs to bring out the best in them, invariably leads to success. When it all comes together, it is a beautiful thing to behold.

I have come across many teams in my career who have overachieved. It was obvious that they were not the most physically talented team on the field that day, yet they found a way to win. Not just that day, but consistently. Through observation and conversations with these athletes and their coaches, it became apparent to me that they were self-motivated. Whether this trait came from their family, friends, teachers, or coaches, they obviously had it. The importance of this to team success cannot be over emphasized.

These are some things I learned about motivation throughout my coaching and teaching career. Hundreds of articles have been written on the topic, but I think I can condense it to a few basic points for our purposes.

Sports psychologists have determined that the two most important needs of athletes are:

1) to have fun, which includes the need for stimulation and excitement.

2) to feel worthy, which includes the need to feel competent and successful.

Different athletes use different types of motivational techniques to keep them dedicated to a sport. It could be social relationships, physical fitness, enjoyment, or goal attainment.

With that in mind, consider what actions you can take as a coach that will positively motivate your athletes? What actions will have the opposite effect? It is important to understand the difference between *extrinsic* and *intrinsic* rewards, and which are more meaningful to your athletes. Trophies, medals, money, and praise are *extrinsic rewards* - that is, they are provided to players by others, or externally. *Intrinsic rewards* are those things that are internally satisfying when players participate in sport, having fun and being successful.

Having fun and feeling competent and successful are intrinsic rewards. Extrinsic rewards, such as recognition from others and trophies, can be powerful motivators; but over time, these rewards may become less valued. The best thing about intrinsic rewards, unlike extrinsic rewards, is that they are self-fueling; that is, you as the coach do not need to provide them. In fact, you cannot provide them. What you can do is create the conditions in practices and games that provide your players with opportunities to attain their own intrinsic rewards. Again, think about your coaching actions. Do you create the conditions that help your athletes experience these intrinsic rewards?

Coaches who are great motivators understand this key to motivating their athletes. They know *they* do not motivate players. Instead, they create the conditions or climate in which players motivate themselves. They skillfully use extrinsic rewards to help build intrinsic motivation. When players fail to achieve the intrinsic rewards of having fun and feeling worthy, they will lose the motivation to play and are likely to quit.

One example that comes to mind took place about mid-season during one of our mediocre years. Some of the players were struggling with motivation. It was obvious we were going to be hard pressed to experience a great deal of extrinsic motivation. Winning games and bringing home trophies was not likely to be used as motivation that year.

The challenge was to use extrinsic rewards to build intrinsic rewards. Since trophies, medals, fame, and money seemed to be out of the question, I resorted to praise, small successes, and perhaps most importantly, having fun. I set up fun challenges during practice. This included team competitions that reinforced fundamentals, with an emphasis on having fun. The competitions were designed so that every member of the team experienced success at some point.

I heaped praise on my players every chance I got. Everyone craves a pat on the back, an encouraging word, or just an old fashioned "atta boy." A season might not provide extrinsic rewards, however, praise and encouragement can certainly be used as rewards. I found ways to motivate my players during good times and bad.

The result was a nice turn around in our season, finishing above .500 in the win-loss column. I believe my effort to provide the players with the opportunity to receive intrinsic rewards led to self-motivation, which in turn led to more success on and off the field.

Once you have the answers to the "why" and "what" questions, you must look at your goals and the aspirations of your players and find a way to put the two together. You must lead them in a direction until they arrive at the destination *you* have chosen for them. There are two key terms here. "Lead" and "your destination." Ultimately, you are the coach, having specific goals you want your team to achieve.

It takes a strong leader to make this happen. You must be passionate and enthusiastic. It is imperative that you love what you are doing, and portray that love to your players every day. If you are not enthusiastic about what you are doing, you are doomed to failure.

It is possible to be an anti-motivator if there is such a word. A coach who does not possess many of the positive traits I have

Motivation

been presenting, can grind a team into the ground. If the players sense you do not care for them, or do not treat them fairly, they will lose their desire to please you. Your communication, body language, and demeanor can turn off players and eventually your entire team. Yelling at players and embarrassing them are two more things that can destroy a player's motivation.

There was a team in our section of the state a few years ago that had the talent to do great things. They were one of the few teams in our small school designation who could put nine skilled players on the field. They could hit, field, pitch and run the bases, yet underachieved. In fact, they underachieved under this coach year after year.

It was obvious to the other coaches in our section that his players did not enjoy playing for this coach. They lacked enthusiasm, hustle, and the drive to win. The more they lost, the more anti-motivational the coach became. His negative body language and constant public criticism of his players demoralized them. They came out for the team because they loved the game and wanted to compete while having fun. Their coach took what should have been a positive experience and ruined it. It was a terrible spiral, and hard to watch. Don't be an anti-motivator.

I absolutely love the challenge of determining how to get the most out of each of my players. When it all comes together, you can just sit back and watch the beautiful efficient machine you have created unfold. It can be difficult when dealing with the modern-day athlete, but it can be done. You will become frustrated from time to time, however, all the setbacks make it that much sweeter when your goal is accomplished.

Play with Joy in Your Heart

I cannot remember where I read about playing with joy in your heart, but it perfectly sums up how the game should be played and coached. As discussed, there is a lot of failure built into the game of baseball. Failure leads to a multitude of negative thoughts and emotions that quite frankly, at times make the game not much fun at all. The truth is, baseball is a beautiful game. The sights, sounds, and smells are like no other. The smell of freshly cut grass, the pop of the ball in the glove, the rhythm and flow of the game are magical.

I worry about kids playing the game today. Do they really enjoy playing? Do they play with joy in their hearts, or are they so focused on winning that they are missing the beauty around them? Do coaches coach with joy in their hearts?

I have witnessed many coaches who don't seem to be having much fun at all. It seems there are so many tournaments and travel leagues, that a lot of the fun has gone out of the game. I read once if you want to see baseball at its best, put a group of kids together, toss them a ball and walk away. The days of pickup games, invisible runners and right field being an automatic out are a thing of the past. In a way, it makes me sad.

The secret is to coach in such a way that your players enjoy the game. This does not mean every practice and game is a free for all without rules or discipline. It simply means there is a way to work hard and have fun at the same time. I think this was one of the things that I did well as a coach. We worked hard. We prided ourselves in outworking our opponents; yet most days, we found a way to laugh and have fun.

One of the best pieces of advice I can give a coach is to be comfortable in your own skin. Have confidence in who you are as a coach and person. Don't take yourself so seriously. Self-deprecation can be a valuable tool in your coaching arsenal. Learn to relax and enjoy your players. Exude confidence and enthusiasm. Your players will mimic your personality more than you think.

The best example I have seen of kids playing with joy in their hearts took place at a showcase I was helping run a few years ago. The showcase was run by College Select Baseball and was one of the best I have witnessed. Like most showcases, college coaches and scouts were in the stands watching us put the players through their paces. Timing the 60-yard dash, infield and outfield plays, along with catcher's pop times. The usual stuff. The uniqueness of this showcase was that they divided the one hundred or so kids into teams and played three seven inning games.

This showcase was very well organized. Each team had their own uniform including numbered jerseys for the coaches and scouts to use as identification. The coaching staff each managed a team once the games began. There was a team from a high school in the New York City area. A diverse group of athletes from a wide variety of backgrounds. They played with more enthusiasm than any team I have ever seen. They hustled, laughed, cheered, obviously thoroughly enjoying the opportunity to play baseball. It was something to see, and something I will never forget. A picture indelibly printed in my mind of playing the game with joy in your heart.

A showcase can be a tense setting for the players. More than likely, their parents or high school coach have strongly encouraged them to attend. They are acutely aware the stands are filled with college coaches and scouts watching their every move. The result can be a nervous, tight performance that does not truly represent the skill of the athlete.

The players from New York City showed none of that. They flowed across the field with a hop in their step and a smile on their faces. Their every move portrayed their love of the game for all to see. What coach or scout would not love to have a player like that on their team? My guess is they made a favorable impression. They also won all three games they played that weekend.

In conclusion, try your best to relax and enjoy the game and your players. Naturally, you will deal with adversity. There will be tough losses, players who challenge your rules, parents questioning your decisions, bad weather, bad calls, and the list goes on. Every one of these is a given. You *will* face adversity. Don't take it personally. It comes with the territory.

The successful coach is the one who takes it all in stride and finds a way to make the game fun. It is important for the coach to coach with joy in his or her heart as well. Remember your love of the game, why you have a passion for the sport, and what inspired you to coach others. Let your players see that side of you. It *will* pay off.

The longer I play this great game, the more I appreciate the chance to step on the field with my teammates. I feel blessed to still be able to compete at the age of sixty-nine. I know each game could be my last, and I treasure them like never before. I can honestly say there is joy in my heart when I play. I have always

Play with Joy in Your Heart

loved and enjoyed the game, but now that I know the end of my playing days are fast approaching, I take the time to enjoy the moment. This is my wish for you and your players.

Pine Valley's Justin Young and D.J. Cortwright celebrate the Panthers 6-2 win Saturday over Brocton.
P-J photo by Mark L. Anderson

Photo courtesy of The Post-Journal

Fear of Failure

I'm often asked, "Why are so many baseball programs going downhill? Why are so few boys playing baseball?" Part of the answer is the popularity of other sports, and of course the many opportunities other than sport available to kids. In our area of the country, participation in all sports is down. Summer leagues and high school sports have seen a drastic decline in participation. Pickup games are a thing of the past. When it comes to sports participation in general, a fair observation is that the current generation of children are less physically active than those of a generation ago. However, this is a blanket statement that does not get to the heart of the issue.

I have a strong opinion regarding this topic when it comes to baseball specifically. This is based on twenty-seven years of observing students in grades K-12 as well as coaching at the Modified, Junior Varsity, and Varsity high school level. We, as parents and teachers, have raised a generation of children who are afraid to fail. Not only are they afraid to fail, they do not even know what failure is. Everyone makes the team and regardless of their skill level, everyone gets to play. Worst of all, everyone gets a trophy. Years ago, we, decided life was just too difficult for our children. Their self-esteem suffered because they were not successful at everything they did. We decided not to bruise their egos, and to protect their feelings, making them successful at everything they attempted.

Lower the standards, give everyone a trophy, and micromanage all relationships. I know we meant well, but we really did our children a disservice. Not to say that failure, pain, and anguish should be a daily occurrence for our little ones, but completely eliminating setbacks is not the way to prepare someone for life. It is a competitive world. Our children will compete for college, jobs, spouses, and a wide variety of things throughout their lives.

This ties directly into my theory of why participation is down in baseball. It is a difficult game to play. Failure is built into every at bat, fielding chance, and pitch thrown. You either make the play, get the hit, steal the base, make the pitch or you don't. Just you, with nowhere to hide, or anyone to blame (well maybe the umpire, but we will talk more about that later). I had a saying on the wall in my office: "Show me a player who is afraid to look bad, and I'll show you a team I can beat every time."

If you get a hit three out of ten times for the length of your career you are going to the Hall of Fame. Where else can you fail seven out of ten times and be a success? Miss seven of ten field goals on the football field and you are quickly looking for a new job. Let in seven of every ten shots on goal in hockey or soccer, and you will quickly be guided to the bench.

That is just how difficult the game of baseball is, and this generation of children struggle handling it. They are not equipped to endure the failure that will eventually lead to success. We face a daunting task. One that we must take on not only as it relates to baseball, but more importantly as it relates to life.

I had a student who was a natural athlete, and an absolute stud of a baseball player. Ryan Sweda played on our Modified team as a seventh grader, leaving the school district returning as a ninth grader. My routine was to place a signup sheet on the

Baseball Is Life Is Baseball

high school coach's office door for both the Junior Varsity and Varsity teams. I noticed Ryan signed up for the Junior Varsity team, which puzzled me, because I was sure he could be a starter on my Varsity team.

I was certain I knew the reason he wanted to stay at the junior varsity level. He was the best player on any team he had ever played on. I saw him play as a seventh grader and he dominated. He played against one of my nephews in a summer league and was the best player on the field by a mile. The thought of him failing was behind his decision. He had experienced nothing but success on the diamond. Quite simply, he was suffering from fear of failure.

The next day, I met with Ryan and tried my best to convince him he could succeed at the varsity level. He was a big strong kid, and it was odd to see his body language and expression project a lack of confidence during our meeting. He did not make eye contact, looking down at his feet and speaking very quietly. Try as I might, he wanted no part of playing at the varsity level.

Next up were his parents. They were very nice people, who obviously wanted what was best for their son. Think of yourself as a parent trying to protect your child from failure and disappointment. I was the father of two girls, and could appreciate their perspective, but I was confident success was in Ryan's future.

I began our meeting explaining my many years of experience and how many high school athletes had crossed my path over the years. I conveyed to them just how talented their son was. In my opinion, he was a rare five tool player meaning he could hit, hit for power, run, field, and throw. He had every skill needed to dominate at the high school level in our league.

They were hesitant at first, but as I continued to sing Ryan's praises, I could see a little crack in their armor. I assured them I would send him down to the junior varsity team if he struggled. I had his best interest at heart as well. I could see in their faces they trusted me. They realized I would put their son's well-being over winning.

I was relieved, but a little concerned as well. What if the pressure was too much? What if, despite his skills, he could not handle it, crashing and burning? The ending to this story is that he exceeded all our expectations. Ryan's four-year career at the varsity level was nothing short of magnificent. He pitched, played first base, and outfield. This young man hit some of the longest home runs I have ever seen. One of his blasts flew over the center field fence landing in the school parking lot bouncing off one of the umpire's cars. In the clutch, he was the guy we wanted at the plate or on the mound. When his high school playing days were over, he held five Career New York State Records. Batting average .486, RBI's 178, hits 156, doubles 47, and home runs, 22. He was selected to the All Western New York Team twice. The icing on the cake was his selection to the New York All State First Team. The first baseball player in school history to achieve this honor.

I was watching a high school basketball team a couple of years ago. This story falls into the category of 'show me a player afraid to fail and I'll show you a team I can beat every time.' I was familiar with the players and coach. They were a talented athletic group. I noticed a pattern as the game progressed.

If a player made a mistake, the coach verbalized his displeasure, called time out and sat the kid on the bench. He re-entered the game shortly thereafter, but the damage had been done. I began paying more attention and noticed that the second a player made a mistake he looked to the bench at his coach.

I dug deeper into what was going on and began to realize the players were not taking any chances at all. They were stiff and cautious, completely stifling their natural ability. They were playing scared. Not afraid of their opponent, but afraid of making a mistake. The result was they lost the game. They were the better team, but were handicapped by their fear of making a mistake. Fear of failure is a powerful thing.

There is a long list of extraordinarily successful people who failed many times before becoming who we know them as today. Walt Disney was fired from the *Kansas City Star* newspaper because the editor told him he lacked imagination and did not have any good ideas. One of Stephen King's most successful books *Carrie* was rejected by thirty publishers. Michael Jordan was cut by his high school basketball coach. We now think of him as one of the greatest basketball players of all time. In our minds he has won multiple championships, and made incredible game winning shots, yet here is one of his quotes. "I have missed more than 9,000 shots in my career. I have lost almost 300 games. On 26 occasions I have been entrusted to take the game winning shot, and I missed. I have failed over and over and over again in my life. And that is why I succeed."

When I think of successful baseball players Mickey Mantle tops my list. A five-tool legend of the game. He hit five hundred thirty-six home runs, won the triple crown, was selected to twenty All-Star teams, and won three MVP awards. There are many more stats cementing his place in baseball history, yet he was quoted as saying he struck out enough times in his career to constitute an entire season. He struck out seventeen hundred ten

Fear of Failure

times in his career, which actually adds up to about three seasons.

We can use sport as a laboratory to teach kids that it is okay to fail. In fact, it is vital that they fail. The failure kids experience in sport will be mirrored in life one way or another. It should be a training ground teaching our children how to set goals, working hard to achieve them, and then keeping at it when things do not go their way. Failure and disappointment are built into the game of baseball and life. Accept it and be strong enough to move on.

So how do you address this in your program? Let's be honest. It is an uphill battle that will not happen overnight. You need a long-term plan when starting a sports program.

Get a clear picture in your head of your program from top to bottom. Set short and long-term goals and follow your plan unwaveringly. The hardest part may be getting kids to come out for your sport. What can you offer them to meet their needs? Be honest. We are going to work hard, have fun along the way, and if you follow my lead, there is an excellent chance you will be successful.

Every child wants to experience success. They want affirmation that they are okay, and they want recognition for their achievements. You are trying your best to meet these needs, but they will have to earn it. There will be ups and downs, but in the end, it will happen, and it will be that much sweeter because it was not automatically given.

It is difficult to create a daily plan to implement this philosophy. Every coach is different. Trying to be something you are not, will not fly with your players. Be yourself. It will take a conscious effort every day to make it happen. This coaching philosophy is bigger than wins or losses. You will be making a major contribution to the future well-being of your players and to society in general. The wins will come as a direct result of implementing the strategies in this book.

I would like you to think about one more thing. If I am right about the state of the current generation of children, how successful can the children you come into contact be if they follow your teachings?

If they are confident, hardworking, and not afraid to fail, the sky is the limit. Many of those with whom they are competing with in life will not have these skills. They do not have to be superstars to be successful in life. Think about how important the coaching profession is. You can change lives in a positive way better than almost any other person your players will encounter in life. My hope is that you accept the challenge.

"It is impossible to live without failing at something, unless you live so cautiously that you might as well not have lived at all, in which case you have failed by default."- J. K. Rowling

Photo courtesy of The Post-Journal

Fear of Failure

Baseball's Best: *All Western New York team*

Outstanding in their field: Kneeling, from left: Tony Kurtz, Newfane; Mark Houck Jr., Lake Shore; Ryan Sweda, Pine Valley; Justin Tedesco, Lew-Port; and Clate Brigham, West Seneca East. Standing: Chris Warner, Orchard Park; Adam Durfee, Williamsville North; Bobby Warne, Albion; Derek Kinder, Albion; and Ryan Dunford, Timon/St. Jude. Not pictured is Paul Wilson, Allegany-Limestone. Baseball honor roll, Page B6.

Photo courtesy of The Post-Journal

Confidence

As a coach, I was always confident we would succeed. The pre-season has its ups and downs. Doubts about the skill level, specific positions, and mental toughness would always find a way to creep into my thoughts. Once we started playing league games, however, I felt we were good enough to win almost every game we played. That is what I believed, and that is the image I projected to my players. I talked to them about it all the time. I wanted them to honestly believe they were good players. Better than their opponents. They had worked hard and deserved to win. I think it is important at this point to mention how important it is for you as the coach to exude confidence. Your body language and mannerisms need to portray confidence. This is most important when things are not going your way. Reflecting on John Wooden's Pyramid of Success, he states, "You must believe in yourself if you expect others to believe in you."

A certain amount of confidence comes from knowing that you have put in the work and have not cut corners. Players have executed the fundamentals of their positions over and over again until they become second nature. Once again, I refer to John Wooden when he states, "You can't have confidence unless you've prepared correctly. Failing to prepare is preparing to fail." You have nurtured them with positive comments and constructive criticism. The stage has been set. This is all well and good, but at some point, individual player confidence must evolve into team confidence.

Confidence

Players must believe that they are good enough to beat any opponent they face. It helps if an event takes place turning this belief into reality. A comeback win against all odds is one of those events that did it for my team.

We started that season losing seven of our eight non-league games. These games did not count toward playoff seedings, but they were important nonetheless. This was the time to put the pieces in place and build momentum for the regular season. We took the field for our first league game looking as if we had lost the game before the first pitch was thrown. Naturally, we lost. The team had talent, but we just could not get it together. I felt as frustrated as I ever have with a team. Something was missing. What was it? How do I right the ship? I had acquired several strategies over the years. Which one was needed at this point in time?

Following the last defeat, I held a team meeting in the locker room. In what I believe was the best motivational speech I ever made, I laid it all on the line. I criticized their lack of commitment and effort. I addressed each player, highlighting how talented they were and why there was no reason we should be losing these games. I challenged them to play to their potential by re-dedicating themselves to the season. The town and the school were counting on them. Let's make them proud. I wish I had recorded that speech because we won thirteen of our last sixteen games from that point on.

We outscored our opponents during that stretch 157-96. Good pitching, solid defense, and timely hitting were the order of the day.

Our team leaders had taken over, inspiring the rest of the players to give it their all. I was both thrilled and a bit surprised that a turnaround could happen so quickly and efficiently. Deep down they wanted to succeed. My players had always taken pride in the school's athletic achievements. I knew they wanted the community to be proud of them. It was a matter of dedicating themselves to that goal. Most importantly, they were having fun. The losses didn't bother me as much as what they were doing to my players. I hated to see them depressed and mentally beaten. Those days were gone.

The winning streak led to a ballgame that ingrained a "never die" attitude into our players and program for years to come.

It was Tuesday, June 3, 1997, and we would play Notre Dame of Batavia, Section V at our local minor league stadium. They were an excellent team, who had worked a little late inning magic of their own to get to this all-important contest. The winner would go on to the state final four with a chance to win the coveted New York State Championship. The losers' season would end.

I was feeling nervous in a good way. The kind of butterflies that tell you you're focused and excited. Which team would show up in our biggest game to date? The bumbling group who struggled to win a game early on, or the confident team that went on a winning streak?

It was a beautiful day. Sunshine and a light breeze accenting the sights and sounds as we took the field for our pre-game warmup. Metal cleats scrapped the cement steps of the dugout as the Pine Valley Panthers took the field. "Let's go boys!" echoed across the field accompanied by well wishes from our large contingent of fans. "Go get 'em." "You've got this." The crack of the wood fungo bounced off the stadium walls as ground ball after ground ball bounded across the infield. "Take one, take one.

Confidence

Thataboy Jeremy. Great scoop over there, Jason. Alright, let's turn two. Look sharp." High fly balls silhouetted against the blue sky followed to the outfield. "Hit the cut, hit the cut. Nice job." Our catcher's voice boomed out ,"Cut two, cut two." Our warmup always ended with me throwing to our catcher who threw to second practicing defending a steal. The rest of the team lined up on the foul line cheering him on. "Come on now, shoot him. Wooooo, nice shot kid."

The sights, smells, and sounds of a ball game about to begin. It is a special feeling. One fraught with a myriad of feelings. Excitement, anticipation, nervousness, and pride that you had made it to this point. I loved these moments. The longtime coach of our beloved Buffalo Bills football team Marv Levy, was often quoted as saying to his teams, "Where would you rather be than right here right now?"

That is exactly how I felt.

These games always begin with a great deal of fanfare. The players and coaches are introduced, lining the third and first base foul lines followed by the playing of the national anthem. I could see the tension on our kids' faces. They were nervous and tight. We always talk about this just being another game, but the moment overwhelmed them. My only hope was that we would get through the first inning and get the butterflies out of our system. It was not to be.

Notre Dame scored three runs in the first inning and seven in the second. Our pitcher, D.J. Cortright, was doing all I could have asked of him other than strike everyone out. A couple of hits were sprinkled in with several routine balls that were botched, as our players fought their nerves. Most coaches would pull their pitcher at this point. None of this was D.J.'s fault. Although things looked grim, and it certainly seemed like we were in big trouble, I left him in the game.

At the end of the second inning, I reminded the players about our winning streak to end the season. There was a lot of baseball to be played. "Let's get on the board boys. Just a run or two this inning to get us going and show them this game is not over. We didn't start this season in March to come here and play two innings." Wouldn't you know it, we scored seven runs the next inning and it was game on.

The more we scored that inning the tighter their team got. They ended up making three errors of their own. We were only down ten to seven. D.J. shut them down over the next three innings as we managed to put one more run on the board. What happened next was something I had never seen before or since.

We managed to get runners on second and third base with two outs. Our batter was a notoriously poor curveball hitter. Notre Dame's scouting report was right on the money. The first pitch was a curveball. Swing and a miss. The second pitch was another curveball with the same result. Would their pitcher make a mistake and try to fool him with a fastball? He was far too smart for that. Here comes the curveball again. I could see it all happening in slow motion. It was a beauty, breaking sharply and bouncing in front of the plate.

Our hitter Derek Smith was committed, taking a mighty swing. The crack of the bat shocked everyone as the ball shot between the shortstop and third baseman scoring two runs. We had tied the game. I remember their third baseman turning and looking at me in the coaching box. All I could do was shrug. Who had seen something like that before?

Confidence

My confidence level skyrocketed with one crazy swing of the bat. I had a bounce in my step as I jogged to the dugout to huddle with my boys. We were fired up. Old "Mo" was on our side.

We scored the go ahead run in the fifth inning with a lead-off walk, sacrifice bunt and a solid hit to score that precious run. D.J. did the rest, shutting them down and not allowing a run after that awful second inning. A slow roller to our first baseman, Jason Reynolds, and the celebration was on. Our outfielders and players in the dugout sprinted toward the mound joining the dogpile of pure joy. The stadium was filled with shouts of congratulations as the parents and fans streamed down from the bleachers and leaned over the back of our dugout. Clapping each other on the back and hugging everyone in sight. "You did it boys, we're so proud of you. I knew you could do it."

Our dejected opponents had lined up ready for the traditional handshake. Heads held low, with little effort to hide their disappointment. Inevitably there were tears in their eyes as their fine season had come to an end. I had seen this same emotion in my players more than once over the years. They were big and strong, but just had their hearts broken and could not hide it. They cared, and that is much better than leaving with a smile on your face ready for summer to begin.

"Come on boys, line it up."

We were sincere in our congratulations to their players and coaches. Although the obligatory "good game, good game, good game" seems trite, we looked everyone in the eye holding the handshake for an extra second or two. Like us, they loved the game of baseball and just missed out on a chance to play in the State Final Four Tournament after holding a ten-run lead.

A comeback for the ages. That victory set the tone for the rest of my coaching career. You are never out of a ballgame. Each team that followed believed that with every fiber of their being.

The local radio broadcast of that game was done by a long-time announcer and good friend Dan Palmer. He put together a montage of his calls of the game to music that gives me goosebumps to this day. He dramatically painted a picture of despair early on, followed by pure joy in the end. I played that tape for every one of my teams after that at our first day of practice. This is who we are. This is what we do. We are the Panthers and we never quit.

State bound

OBSERVER Photo by Mort Buss Jr.
D.J. Cortright, who pitched a complete game, shows his relief after Pine Valley won the Far West Regional title in the high school baseball playoffs held Tuesday at Jamestown Community College. Pine Valley progresses to the state semifinals in Herkimer. STORY ON PAGE B1.

Photo courtesy of The Post-Journal

Umpires

Like all of us, umpires come in all different shapes and sizes. I am referring to skill set and personality here rather than physical size and shape. Some are good at what they do, and some not so much. For some, it is all about them. They are there to run the show, exerting their authority at every opportunity. A good umpire is one you hardly notice.

I made a point of getting along with umpires. It was made clear to me early in my career, that arguing and showing an umpire up was never productive. The more you argued, the worse things got for your team. I never met an umpire who relented to a coach's rantings. That is not entirely true. There are times a young inexperienced umpire would give in to the pressure, but is that how you want to win a game?

My approach was to be cordial from the time they took the field until they left. This is not to say I never disagreed with their calls. However, I did so in a way that did not show them up. My style was to wait for the inning to end and approach the umpire casually, facing the outfield away from the fans. The conversation might be, "What did you see on that play Jim?" He might respond, "I saw the tag before he reached the base." My response might be, "From my angle, I saw his foot beat the tag." Followed by, "Okay, thanks for the explanation."

The umpire knew I disagreed with his call, but also appreciated that I did so in a courteous manner. Making a scene serves no purpose in this scenario. The fans would give him enough of an earful anyway. There were times the fans demanded a more vocal response from me, but I did not want to burn bridges. It paid off in the long run.

One example that comes to mind took place in a Far West Regional game. This is the game that either ends your season or sends you to the State Final Four Tournament. We were facing an excellent team from another section. They were a Catholic school, and as such, typically recruited talented players. A luxury not available to public schools.

We battled them toe to toe for five innings. With a man on third base and two outs, our pitcher began his delivery home. The plate umpire half raised his hand indicating time was called. Our pitcher stopped his delivery and was immediately called for a balk by the base umpire. He waved the go ahead run home. I clearly saw what happened but was feeling apprehensive as the umpires were from their section not mine. Would that make a difference today? Could we talk this out?

I called time, and politely asked the base umpire if he could confer with the home plate umpire explaining what I saw. My body language was non-confrontational, trying to remain professional in the moment. The umpire appeared to be in the same mode and agreed to discuss the situation with his counterpart. After a brief conference he reversed his decision.

To say this changed the game would be an understatement. I'm certain they would not have entertained my request had I come unglued. We got the last out to end the inning and the threat. The game was lost in the tenth inning on a seeing eye single and a bang, bang play at the plate. A tough loss, but a very well-played ball game by two outstanding teams.

I received a call from my brother-in-law Dan Sadowski on the bus ride home. He is a big baseball fan, who religiously followed our team. He said, "Now I have seen everything. How in the world did you get that umpire to change his call?" It made me feel good that my core values came through for my team in a critical situation. I have never been a confrontational person on or off the field.

I see many of the umpires who officiated my high school games now that I am playing in a local senior league. We remain great friends to this day. I enjoy the camaraderie we share. We take the field as player and umpire, able to take part in the greatest game on earth as colleagues, not adversaries.

Control What You Can Control

Controlling what you can control is one of the most important concepts to get your players to understand. It is easy to preach, yet difficult to put into action. It takes a great deal of mental training and toughness for your athletes to understand and internalize this important piece of the puzzle.

Like life, sports have a tremendous number of variables that are completely out of our control. Time spent worrying about these things hinders your performance as an athlete, coach, and as an everyday person. It is impossible to get into the "zone" if you are distracted by negative thoughts focusing on anything other than the task at hand. I have seen athletes go completely off the rails because of an umpire's call or an error by a teammate. A bad bounce, gust of wind, poor field conditions, coaching decisions, and a wide variety of issues that are simply out of your control should not impact your performance in a negative way.

You have a job to do as a pitcher, hitter, fielder, and base runner. Focus on the process and do your job. One of my favorite sayings when an athlete would complain about something out of their control is, "Nobody cares." Perhaps a bit harsh, but it was to drive home the point that it is out of your control. Stop making excuses. Focus on the next pitch.

An excellent read is *Heads Up Baseball* by sport psychologist Dr. Ken Ravizza. He spends a great deal of time on the topic of controlling what you can control and learning to control yourself. He emphasizes two key fundamentals:

Control What You Can Control

1) You can't control what happens around you, but you can control how you respond.

2) You must be in control of yourself before you can control your performance.

Don't get the impression that nothing else going on around you matters. Of course, it does; but these are only *concerns*. How the other team plays, the decisions your coach makes, how your team plays in the field and at the plate are all parts of the game and things you consider. However, your energy needs to be spent on the things you personally can control. Most importantly, you are in control of how you respond to all these concerns. Keeping your thoughts positive when things are going poorly around you is difficult, but critical to success.

The odds are you have acquired a habit of reacting negatively. This is simply human nature. Habits are hard to break; however, through training and repetition, they can be broken. The repetition must be purposeful. If you are trying to change your swing, you do not blindly take 100 swings as fast as you can. You break it down, taking purposeful quality swings. Always quality over quantity. Practice eliminating negative thoughts. The challenge is getting to the point that they either do not enter your head or are quickly pushed out if they do.

When recalling past games, what is your focus? Are you feeding your fears by harping on the negative by recalling times you failed, or are you making conscious and strategic efforts to focus on what you did well to increase your confidence? When you do acknowledge shortcomings, are you analyzing your progress towards goals and making definitive plans for growth, or are you dwelling on circumstances beyond our control?

You must be in control of yourself before you can control your performance. I cannot emphasize enough the importance of this concept. Greg Maddux comes to mind when I imagine an example of what self-control looks like. He pitched in the Big Leagues for twenty-three seasons, winning three hundred fifty-five games. Perhaps his best season was in 1995 with the Atlanta Braves. He recorded nineteen wins that year, throwing ten complete games with an ERA of 1.63. The master of control, Maddux only walked twenty-three batters while striking out one hundred eighty-one.

The master of control moniker also applies to his demeanor on the mound. He never got rattled. If the camera zoomed in on his face after a pitch, you would never know if it was a ball, strike, homerun, or groundout. He controlled his thoughts which led to his masterful control of the baseball.

Dustin Johnson on the PGA Tour is another example of someone who understands the concept of controlling what you can control. As of this writing, he has won twenty-four PGA Tournaments including the Masters and U.S. Open. Like Maddux his facial expression and body language never seem to change. He has accepted the fact that certain things are out of his control, and he moves on.

They are true professionals who have mastered the art of self-control and playing the game one pitch or shot at a time. It is their self-control that allows them to perform at an elite level against the best players on the planet. They seem to be free of tension and doubt. They have allowed their natural abilities to take over free of negative thoughts. They are masters of controlling what they can control.

The 'control what you can control' concept is one of the most valuable skills you can possess. Stress has a tremendous negative impact on your mind and body. Emotionally, it can cause depression, anxiety, a lack of motivation and focus, racing thoughts, constant worry, feeling overwhelmed, and a lack of concentration. Project those emotions onto a ball field or your everyday life, and you can see the damage stress can cause.

Stress is the cause of many physical ailments as well affecting the heart, intestinal tract, blood pressure, sleep, and muscle tension and pain. Again, this is not what you need on the diamond or in everyday life.

With a family history of ulcers and stress related disorders, I have tried my best to eliminate stress from my life. I rarely feel stress on the ball field, whether playing or coaching. That is where I'm most comfortable. I understand the nuances of the game, and things that are in or out of my control.

It is more difficult in my everyday life, although I must say it has come easier with age. I have learned to surround myself with people who are positive. I have also learned to not care quite so much about what others think of me.

There are so many opportunities for stress to take control of you throughout the day. Work, traffic, deadlines, family squabbles, accidents, and so much more. It is impossible to eliminate all stress from your life, but you can shorten the list with practice.

The biggest thing you are in control of is YOU. Charles R. Swindoll wrote, "We cannot change the inevitable. The only thing we can do is play on the one string we have, and that is our attitude. I am convinced that life is 10% what happens to me and

90% of how I react to it. And, so it is with you....we are in charge of our Attitudes."

Postgame Learning

You have read a lot of information to this point. Like many books on the topic, it has focused on pre-game and game day strategies. What happens after the game can also help you become a better coach and help your athletes become better players.

Great coaches and players are constantly learning. There is a great deal to be learned after the game. This is the time to reflect upon and evaluate your performance. What went right? What went wrong? Most importantly, why? Analyzing what you did right will be a big boost to your confidence. Analyzing what you did wrong that day will help you correct your mistakes. You need to be honest in your evaluation. No excuses. If you are the coach, how did you manage the game and your players? Try to include all parts of the game from start to finish. How was your pre-game preparation? Did you scout your opponent? Did you incorporate their strengths and weaknesses into your game plan? How did you handle adversity? Did you exude confidence and communicate with your players positively, or did your body language show the opposite? Were you in control of your thoughts and emotions? Evaluate the decisions you made - bunting, stealing, pinch running, defensive alignment, pitching changes. Develop a self-survey and complete it after the game.

If you are a player, rate your performance as well. How was your pre-game routine? What was your mindset? Were you focused? Did you play the game one pitch at a time? How did you handle adversity? What could you have done differently? Grade your performance in each category. Use a scale from 1-10.

The post-game survey and self-reflection is a tool to not only evaluate your performance, but to develop a plan to improve the areas that need improving. If you were unable to re-focus after things didn't go your way, what mental skill must you review to improve? Hopefully by now you have a full arsenal of strategies at your disposal.

I think the hardest part of postgame learning is being honest with yourself. This is not the time to play the blame game. Wait until all the dust has settled and no one is around. Eliminate your emotions and any preconceptions you may have. Analyze each component of your performance that day. Most importantly, develop a plan to improve.

This is a life skill as well. We live in a fast-paced world. Faster than it has ever been, and it is still accelerating. People pulling at us in all directions, social media, cable news, streaming shows, non-stop texting. It has become more difficult to find a little quiet time to think about and evaluate your day. I strongly suggest making time to do just that. Think of it as "post day" learning. How did you handle your day? What could you have done to make it a little more stress free?

I interact with many groups in and out of baseball. My days are filled, and usually fast paced. However, I always find time to relax and think. Putting on the brakes and clearing my mind for the next day. It has made all the difference for me.

Post Game Evaluation

Scale of 1-10   1 being lowest score and 10 highest

	1	2	3	4	5	6	7	8	9	10
I was mentally prepared to play										
I felt confident in my ability										
I showed good body language										
I was a good teammate										
I played the game one pitch at a time										
I only tried to control what was in my control										
I hustled										
I showed enthusiasm										
I exhibited good sportsmanship										
I was in control of my emotions										
I was focused for the entire game										

What I learned about myself today -

Things I would have done differently -

My strengths -

My weaknesses -

My plan to get better -

The Mental Side of the Game

There is no doubt in my mind that the single most important factor in taking a good team to the next level is the mental side of the game. I observed it firsthand the year we won the New York State High School State Championship.

I had built a strong program over the years, implementing the strategies presented in this book. Good communication, discipline, coaching for character and, of course, solid baseball fundamentals. We won several league and sectional championships, but could never get to the big dance and win it all.

I first became aware of this critical component to success, while playing with several former Major League players in Senior League tournaments around the country. I was fortunate enough to be on pitching staffs with Bill "Spaceman" Lee, Jerry Reuss, Dave Von Ohlen, Mark Bomback, and Jim Bouton to name a few. Sorry about the name dropping, but it is an integral part of the story. These were players who had played at the highest level of the game and had been extraordinarily successful. I fully expected their physical skills to be superior to us amateurs, what surprised me, was their mental approach to the game. It was eye opening to say the least.

They had mastered the art of playing the game one pitch at a time. Whether they threw a filthy breaking ball to strike out the number four hitter, or hung a curveball giving up a homerun to the number nine hitter, all that mattered was the next pitch. They lived in the present. Trying to control what they could control. They never made excuses. The weather, the field conditions, a

The Mental Side of the Game

fielding error, an umpire's call, were all just part of the game. No different than the foul line or home plate. Everything rolled off their backs. They focused on the task at hand with unwavering clarity.

I think this story illustrates my point. I was playing with a team from the Boston area that included Dave Von Ohlen. Dave had a nice career in the Big Leagues, playing for St. Louis, Cleveland, and Oakland over a five-year span. Throughout the six games of pool play leading up to the playoffs, Dave never threw a ball. He hung out with us at team meals and outings, sat in the dugout every game and cheered us on, but I never saw him throw a ball. I cannot remember exactly how old he was at the time, but he had been out of pro ball for several years.

Finally, his time came. He was to pitch our first playoff game. Naturally, my curiosity was piqued. Who was this guy, and what could he do for us? There I was a short distance away spying on him as he entered the bullpen. He started gently lobbing the ball to the catcher, as we all do, and finally signaled for the catcher to crouch. He threw three warmup pitches that missed the mark. Now when I say missed the mark, they were maybe six inches off target at most.

What came next was my first 'ah ha' moment about mental conditioning. Dave held the ball in his glove and turned his back to the catcher with his head down and eyes closed for about fifteen seconds. When he turned around and started throwing, the catcher's mitt barely moved pitch after pitch. What just happened? What sort of magic was this?

The conclusion to this story is that he threw a complete nine inning game using only eighty-three pitches. He was absolutely masterful on the mound. One of the best pitching performances

I have had the pleasure to witness. A true professional. From that point on, I started picking the brain of every professional player I came across about their mental preparation.

The seed had been planted. I began to research articles and attend clinics on the subject. The more people I talked to, and the more I read, the more I realized I had stumbled onto something particularly important. This was the ingredient I had been missing. Sure, I had heard about visualization and meditating, but this was much more sophisticated. I began to understand the basic concepts, and the strategies to put these ideas into practice. I learned about how the brain functions when dealing with stressful situations, and how it affects physical performance. I learned specifically how to play the game one pitch at a time. Most importantly I learned how to deal with failure.

There is so much failure built into in the game of baseball. It is a given that your player *will* fail. It is the nature of the game. I often refer to the quote by Tom Hanks in the movie *A League of Their Own*. "It's supposed to be hard. If it wasn't hard everyone would do it. The hard is what makes it great." Baseball beats you down mentally. It can be cruel at times, making you question your abilities like no other sport. It takes a mentally strong person to endure the slings and arrows. The great ones know this and have trained their minds to overcome adversity.

What if you could bring some of these skills to your players? What kind of edge would you have over your opponents? I did, and I am here to tell you, it indeed gave us an edge. It's not easy. Not everyone will buy in at first. In fact, some of your players may never buy in. Eventually though, players using these techniques will see improvement in their overall play. This is what happened with my team. Before long, those players who rejected the idea

The Mental Side of the Game

and were struggling jumped on board. Who isn't looking for an edge?

I think it is important at this point to discuss why meltdowns happen and why mental training is necessary. We can see the symptoms of a meltdown as I will discuss below, but what is going on inside the athlete's head? The answer is much more than you can imagine. Fear of failure, embarrassment, insecurity, low self-worth. Many times, an athlete ties his self-worth to his performance on the field.

I drilled into my player's heads that we were not defined by the scoreboard. Wins, losses, errors, or homeruns did not define us as people. All these thoughts running through the players head creates pressure. The pressure creates more negative thoughts and the vicious cycle has begun.

Why not just tell yourself to stop the negative thoughts and actions? Simple, right? Many years of experiences have created a default system. It is this default system that is keeping you from attaining a peak state of mind. One that will not allow you to perform your best under pressure and adversity. Mental practice allows you to re-program your mind to a new default system. It allows you to have a clear mind that is relaxed, and process oriented rather than consequence oriented. I stress breaking the performance down to a process. Hit the mitt rather than strike him out. Have a quality at bat rather than get a hit. The goal is to detach yourself from the outcome. It takes practice to create a new default system.

Let me give you one example of the things I learned and incorporated into my practices and games. These come from Brian Cain. I first saw Brian at a coach's clinic many years ago.

He has since become well known in his field, working with professional and amateur athletes in a wide variety of sports.

One of the things he did was break down a performance into a series of three phases. These phases replicated a stop light. There were green, yellow and red components to it. Green meaning the athlete is firing on all cylinders. Yellow represents some things are going wrong and performance is beginning to suffer. Red means the athlete has lost his focus and is crashing and burning.

Let's use a pitcher as an example. He is on the mound and everything is going his way. He is hitting the corners and getting the calls from the umpire. His fielders are playing flawless defense behind him, and his team is scoring runs. Life is good. Before long, he throws a perfect three-two pitch on the corner, and the umpire calls ball four. Not that big a deal. A little upsetting, but we can assume the light is still green. The runner steals second base and the catcher throws the ball into center field. The next batter bloops a ball into right field driving home a run. Suddenly the light turns yellow. Negative thoughts are creeping into the pitcher's head, "If only I had gotten that called third strike the inning would have been over. Why did Jeff make such a bad throw to second?"

You get the picture. These negative thoughts are now affecting his performance. Before long he hits a batter, walks another, and gives up another hit. Now he is in a red light situation for sure. The game has sped up, and he is no longer in control of his emotions. You better go get him.

The strategy in this situation is to recognize when the light changes from green to yellow and having the ability to get back to green again. This is what good athletes do. There are definite signs that the light is changing if you know what to look for. In the case of a pitcher, he speeds up his movements between pitches. He might begin talking to himself, looking into the dugout. His body language portrays someone who is in a state of frustration, confusion, or defeat.

Fielders have the same cues that things are about to go south. They boot a ball and slump their shoulders, look to the sky, examine their glove, or kick the dirt. Yelling out "refocus" or "separate" is not going to change a thing. You need a plan to get your player back on track. In the case of a pitcher, one strategy is to call time out, stepping off the mound onto the grass. The green grass is a physical cue. Take a deep breath, flush the last pitch, get back on the mound and compete. It is not as simple as it sounds, but if you have put this in place through repetitions during your pre-season practices, it will work. There are pre-pitch techniques, incorporating a deep breath and visualization. There are also physical cues for hitters in the batter's box and fielders as well.

I think most coaches understand the importance of a pre-game routine. Get to a game early and you will see a team stretch and throw. They will take infield and outfield practice and huddle up for a big "one two three team" or whatever the saying of the day is. I strongly believe in pre-game routines. It creates a mindset that prepares your players to play the game. What about a mental pre-game routine? The big difference between the physical pre-game routine and the mental is that the mental falls directly on the player. The coach may have incorporated mental training into his practices and team meetings, but come game time, it now falls on you to mentally prepare for what is to come.

The goal of pre-game mental preparation is to fill your mind with positive thoughts. Visualize yourself hitting line drives all over the field, turning double plays or throwing perfect pitches one after another. Close your eyes and see these things as vividly as possible. Set some time aside away from your teammates in a quiet place and take ten minutes to go through your mental positive thoughts' routine. I made a point of teaching my players to incorporate positive language in their preparation. Eliminate the negative. "I can't do this," is not an acceptable thought or verbalization. Rather, "I will get better if I keep working hard."

Take a step backward and choose a moment in time or a physical action that signals it is game time. Time to put the day aside and focus all your energy on the game. It might be putting on your uniform, or the national anthem. Maybe it is a physical barrier you cross like the gate leading to your field or taking that last step off the bus. A specific thing that flips the switch from student, boyfriend, king of social media to ballplayer.

This is a critical component when it comes to starting the mental process allowing you to be your best that day. Now it is game time. Hopefully, nothing else will clutter your mind. One of the things I love about baseball is for those two and a half hours, nothing else creeps into my brain. What happened earlier in the day is left behind and will be waiting for me when I leave the field. You need to teach your players this technique.

I developed a sheet of positive self-talk that I would give to my starting pitcher the day of the game. My goal was to instill confidence in him while eliminating negative thoughts. I would have him read it to himself slowly ten times about an hour before the game. It might be on the bus or maybe just before we took the field for pre-game warmups at home. Each one specifically tailored to that player. I would then have him find a spot where he was completely isolated 15 minutes before the game and read it ten more times.

Here is one of the examples I used:
Today is the day I have waited for.
My senior year and a go-home game.
I am more than ready.
I have worked hard for this moment.
I am confident.
I have not cut corners. I will be victorious.
I WILL be focused.
I WILL play the game one pitch at a time.
I **WILL** dominate today.
No need to overthrow.
No need to be extra special.
My every day stuff is more than enough to win today.
Today I will shine.
I am tenacious.
Nothing can distract me from my job.
Umpires…Opponents…Bounces…Errors…Weather…all meaningless.
I am mentally stronger than anyone on the field.
Today I show everyone that I cannot be beaten.
I am a warrior and victory will be mine!!!!!

Silly? Maybe, but the results were nothing short of amazing. Now the player in this example was an excellent pitcher. This sheet did not add ten miles per hour to his fastball. However, this was a huge game and he needed to be at his best. That day he shut out an undefeated team, sending us to the New York Final Four Tournament.

You owe it to yourself to expand your horizons and dig into the mental side of baseball. You will find that your players enjoy the thought of doing something their opponents are not doing.

They love an edge. The good news is, there are hundreds of books, articles, and videos on the subject. It will seem overwhelming at first, but soon you will learn to pick out a couple of things that make sense to you and go from there. You may read a book and only come away with two practical ideas for your program. Those two ideas may be just the thing you need to take the next step.

Think about the application of mental training in your everyday life. You can apply the green light, yellow light, red light analogy off the field as well. You start your day refreshed and ready to go. A nice shower followed by a hearty breakfast and off to work you go. Green light mentally, and as you start your ride, green lights physically. As you turn onto the expressway, you come to a standstill as an accident has taken place. Not that big a deal. You left in plenty of time. As your cushion of time slowly expires, you are feeling a bit anxious. It's a big day at work and you don't want to be late. After another five minutes of sitting still, your check engine light comes on. Coincidentally, it's yellow. You have now officially left the green light zone and mentally entered the yellow light zone. Negative thoughts enter your head as all the possible bad scenarios dance around inside your brain.

Traffic begins to flow, and you finally arrive at your job. Running late, you quickly exit your vehicle as the papers for your presentation fall and blow across the parking lot. You are now in a full-blown red light mental state. Totally frustrated, and

The Mental Side of the Game

nowhere near where you need to be mentally to face the day. You are in no condition to perform at your best this morning.

Incorporate some of the strategies I have discussed to get back to your green light and face the day. Execute the mental part of your game.

Mental skills like physical skills must be practiced daily. "We are what we repeatedly do. Excellence then, is not an act, but a habit." - Aristotle

Here are some of my personal favorites:

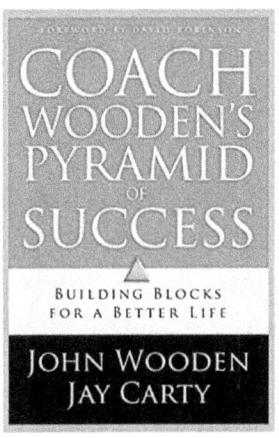

L-R Bill "Spaceman" Lee, Jim Bouton, Charlie LaDuca
Author family photo

Charlie LaDuca and Bill Lee, Sedona Arizona Golf Resort
Author family photo

Charlie LaDuca and Jerry Reuss, MSBL World Series
I'm the short one
Author family photo

Stephen McCoy

I thought about inserting this story into a chapter, finally deciding to let it stand alone. In retrospect, based on the impact this event had on me as a coach and person, it makes sense.

Stephen McCoy was a nice kid. He was a student in my physical education class when I first began my teaching career. Stephen was quiet and a bit shy, and to be perfectly honest, not someone you would characterize as an athlete. He approached me in his senior year and asked if he could try out for the baseball team. Remember, we were a small school. My average number of players on the roster was thirteen and I rarely needed to make cuts.

I told Stephen of course he was welcome to try out. He wrote his name on the signup sheet, showing up at tryouts ready to go. It was obvious Stephen did not have the skill set to play varsity baseball. The junior varsity team was not an option, as seniors were not permitted to play. After three days of tryouts which included every player that signed up, I sat the kids down, made a little speech, and said the team rosters would be posted the next day.

Two sheets were posted on the door. One listing the players who had made the Varsity team, and the other for the Junior Varsity team. Every player who tried out made one of the two teams that year, as was the case most years. I pulled Stephen aside and explained his role on the team.

I would do my best teaching him the fundamentals of the game and getting him playing time whenever the opportunity arose. The only thing I asked of him was not to be a distraction. Becoming upset with playing time and disrupting the team was not an option. He agreed and stuck to his promise.

In those days in New York State, we were allowed to play a maximum of twenty-four games prior to playoffs. Our league schedule that year was twelve games, meaning we could add an additional twelve non-league games. These were games played against opponents outside of our league. I always tried to schedule teams from a higher division, as our goal was to win a state title. We would face stiff competition, and I wanted to be prepared. I used these games to evaluate each player's strengths and weaknesses as well as giving my second-string players a chance to take the field.

Coaches can be placed in two broad categories. Win oriented or athlete oriented. I was extremely competitive and hated to lose. However, I was acutely aware of the needs of every player on my team. I could not in good conscience ask a kid to attend every practice and never set foot on the diamond. I had taught them as young boys, knew their parents and grandparents, and genuinely cared for them. Stephen did get playing time. Granted, not a great deal, but he contributed to our success that year. The highlight was driving in a run in one of our non-league games.

Now as luck would have it, this was the year we had our big comeback win in the Far West Regional game and were headed to our first New York State Final four tournament. This was a big deal. Our girls' basketball team went on an incredible run of State Championship victories. Seven to be exact. They began a tradition of a grandiose farewell from the school as they departed for the big game. Fire trucks from our local fire and rescue department lined up in front of a luxurious coach bus at the front of the school. The entire student body made a gauntlet from the front door of the school to the bus. The girls would walk the gauntlet as the students cheered them on. Once aboard, the fire trucks sounded their horns and sirens and led a procession out of town.

Naturally, we received the same treatment, which led to one of my proudest and most emotional moments in thirty years of coaching. Our players began the proud walk toward the bus soaking in the cheers and well wishes. I was at the end of the line having checked to make sure nothing was left behind. Who was directly in front of me, but Stephen McCoy. The boy who had never won a sports letter or been part of a high school team. The boy who did everything I asked him to do was now reaping the rewards of a job well done.

The students and faculty cheered wildly as we walked toward the bus. What a moment. Shouts of, "Great job boys, make us proud, bring home that trophy," rose above the clapping and air horn blasts from the fire trucks. As I followed closely behind Stephen, he was being clapped on the back as someone shouted, "Go get 'em, Stephen." I teared up and had all I could do to not start bawling right there in front of everyone.

We boarded the bus and headed down the school driveway led by our proud firefighters, sirens blaring and lights flashing announcing to everyone that we were on our way to the biggest game of our lives. As the school faded from sight, I took a moment to let it all sink in. The look of joy and excitement on the faces of the players and coaches affirmed my belief that baseball was the greatest game of all. Given the privilege to coach and teach these kids was a blessing beyond belief.

While thinking about this story, as I mentioned earlier, I could not decide on a chapter or theme for it. So why did I include it in the book? I think it symbolizes all that is good about coaching. The tremendous impact you can have on a person's life. I'm certain Stephen will never forget that day nor will I. I had a lump in my throat just writing this. His memory will not be of getting the game winning hit or making a defensive gem that saved the day. Stephen never did get into the big game. In fact, it was a game to forget as we were trounced twenty-two to one. The love that was sent his way that day, and the pride he must have felt was priceless. It made me realize how trivial the scoreboard was.

Charlie LaDuca High Fiving Stephen McCoy Pre-Game Ceremony
First NYS Final Four Appearance
Photo courtesy of The Post-Journal

The New York State Championship

How It All Came Together

The culmination of all the hard work over the years was winning the New York State Championship. The physical and mental training paid off on that amazing Saturday, June 9th at Conlon Field in Binghamton, New York. The concepts of every chapter in this book played a role in the greatest day in Pine Valley baseball history.

If ever there was to be a year, this was it. We had a strong team with excellent pitching, good hitting, solid fielding, and a mature attitude. There had been many good teams in the past, but I felt our mental game was at an all-time high that year. We went undefeated in league play with a 14-0 record. Overall, we were 18-2 when you count our non-league games. Playoffs take things to an entirely new level, as they are single elimination games. One bad outing and your season is over. The tension builds as the seeding system ensures that each team you play is better than the one you just faced.

Our program was successful, winning more than our share of games as well as numerous league and sectional titles. We had made back-to-back trips to the State Final Four Tournament ten years prior to this season. In both instances we were soundly beaten in the semi-final game. In my twenty years of coaching at Pine Valley we were unable to win the biggest game of all.

The New York State Championship

Then something happened that changed everything and took things to an entirely new level. Something so powerful that I didn't just *think* we were good and would win, but I positively *knew* it. Sadly, the event that opened my eyes and mind to this powerful thought process was a tragedy.

Tim Sercu was a student who I had taught from kindergarten through sixth grade. He joined the varsity baseball team as a sophomore. Tim was a coach's dream. He was a student of the game, who worked hard every day to become a better player. He loved the game of baseball and his teammates, as evidenced by the big smile on his face each time he took the field.

Three years after Tim graduated, his father found him unresponsive in his room one morning. He had been having heart related issues and been seen by several doctors. On the morning of December 13, 2006, his big beautiful heart stopped beating, and he left us. His death hit me very hard. Tim played the game with joy in his heart. Memories of the years teaching him in our elementary school, mixed with flashes of his fielding and hitting, flooded my senses. Tim grew about four inches his junior year. The growth spurt made him clumsy at times as he played in the field. He would frequently take a tumble fielding a ball, yet always found a way to get back up and make the play. We would joke about it, knowing he was in on it and took no offense. That's just the way he was. A smiling, funny, hard-working kid who loved baseball and his teammates. At his funeral, several players were looking to me for answers. What do you tell seventeen and eighteen-year-old kids at such a time? I told them nothing can change what happened, but we could all learn something from it.

I said, "Life is short, and you never know when it will end. There are no guarantees. Go home and give the ones you love an extra hug and stop taking life for granted. Live life to the fullest. Enjoy it. Embrace it with no regrets." I meant those words with all my heart. I am not sure they were very consoling. It was the best I could do. It had only been three years since Tim led our team to a tremendous season as a senior. His memory was fresh in all our minds.

We retired his jersey, hanging it on a wall by our trophy case along with a picture of him in uniform and a quote, "The heart of a Panther never dies." No Pine Valley player would ever wear number 19 again.

From the first practice that season I had a strong sense that Tim was watching over us. I swear there were times I could feel him around me. I don't know what your religious beliefs are, or how you feel about these things, I can only tell you what I felt. I just know that in my mind, he was there every step of the way. I had the strongest sense that no matter what happened, we were going to win the State Championship. Mind you, this was my twenty-first year of coaching. My goal every year was to win the State Championship.

We had some excellent teams over the years and as mentioned, could not get past the NYS semi-final game. Not even close. We were soundly beaten both times. Thinking about winning the title was nothing new, but this was different. I believed with every fiber of my being that nothing could stop us from winning that year. Nothing was going to stop us from achieving the ultimate goal for a high school team. Not the weather. Not injuries. Not disciplinary issues. Not the schedule. Not the umpires. Not our opponents. Nothing. It was a done deal.

The New York State Championship

Many things went wrong that season. In fact, as many or more than I remembered in my twenty-one years of coaching. The difference was that none of it mattered. We laughed about it. We talked about it every day. Every negative became a positive. It only made us stronger. Whether it was a seemingly insurmountable deficit during a game, a bad call by an umpire, or our bus breaking down on the way to the State tournament that led to us missing our scheduled practice that day. Nothing mattered. They were just obstacles for us to leap over on our way to the Championship.

Looking back, it still amazes me at some of the obstacles we had to overcome on our way to the Championship. I had both knees replaced two months prior to the start of the season. I was a bit young for this procedure at the age of 55, but forty-five years of playing ball and pitching had finally taken its toll. I had played baseball right up until that point in local Senior Leagues as well as traveling around the country playing in tournaments. Normally I would run with the team, throw BP, hit and demonstrate all the skills. I continued to do that (minus the running), but at a much slower pace. This was the first event I used as a positive.

I was a good ball player in my day, and it was hard for me not to be able to do the things I had always done as an active coach. I gave it my best shot every day, but the kids could see I was in pain. I would constantly remind them how lucky they were to be young and healthy. They should never take that for granted. What I wouldn't give to have their legs and be able to sprint again. Nobody had an excuse when it came to conditioning. Shortly after that, I began to have soreness in my joints and extreme fatigue. My energy levels had been rapidly declining to the point, but now was having a hard time keeping my eyes open throughout the day.

This was not good timing, as a typical day involved getting out of bed at 5:00 a.m. to work on my wood bat business before heading to school to teach. A full day of teaching was followed by practice or a game, which meant getting back home anywhere from eight to nine thirty at night. A quick dinner, a few more hours on the computer working my small wood bat business, and then off to bed. I finally went to my doctor, who diagnosed my illness as Parvovirus. A nasty little virus that normally afflicts young children. I was unfortunate enough to have never contracted it as a child. In most children, the symptoms are mild and need little treatment. In adults, it is a different story. To make a long story short, there is really nothing they can do. It must run its course. So, there I was with bad knees and anything but a bundle of energy. However, the show must go on, so I had to suck it up.

As I write this, it seems like I'm feeling sorry for myself and making excuses. Not at all. I practiced what I preached. It is important to lead by example. I had a job to do and was not looking for pity. Every one of my players had a legitimate chance to make excuses at some point during the season. My core philosophy was to focus on the goal at hand brushing everything else aside. That is what I did because it was the right thing to do.

We had our usual share of setbacks involving players that season. A little discipline here and there due to academics, but nothing major in that department. We did, however, lose our starting shortstop and #2 pitcher for five weeks due to a rule violation from the previous basketball season. He was involved

The New York State Championship

in a prank gone bad, and given the maximum sentence (well-deserved, I might add).

This was a big blow to the team. It could have been very demoralizing. Instead, it turned into a positive as a couple of players stepped up to fill the void. The bottom line was that by the time he rejoined the team, we had developed another outstanding pitcher who played a big role in the State Tournament. So once again the mindset was, "Okay, no big deal; it will just make us stronger as it was meant to do." It was a necessary setback purposely put there to take us where we wanted to go.

Like all High School teams in the east, spring is a brutal time to get focused and stay focused on baseball. There are so many distractions and interruptions. Besides the obvious weather conditions there are spring vacations, school trips, parties, and on and on and on. For our school, it is the Senior Trip, followed by the Science Trip, then the prom, the musical, and an unending list of obligations other than baseball. It takes a special group, and some real hard work on the part of the coach, to brush this all aside and get back to business. Nothing can change it, control what you can control, so just go with the flow, and make it one more hurdle to overcome.

I used to fight it tooth and nail, but during that magical season, I was at peace with it all because I knew it just didn't matter. I guess that is the best way to describe my frame of mind that season now that I think about it - at peace. I could not help projecting this image to the team because it is the way I truly felt every day.

I could list all the specific things that went wrong that season, but you get the point. I do think, however, two are worth mentioning. The first one took place during our run through the playoffs. We had won our Sectional Championship game beating an excellent team and were moving on to the Far West Regional game. The game was hosted by the Sectional Champions from another region. The winner of this game would advance to the State Final Four. The game was to be played on a Monday at a Minor League Stadium.

The timing was perfect because our pitching rotation was right where I wanted it to be. Our opponents, however, could not throw their ace, as he was out of innings according to sectional pitching regulations. Advantage us. We were all set to go when we got word that the game had been postponed because a heavy rain the night before had washed out the field. This was a bit odd. It was a Minor League field with an infield tarp.

I made some inquiries and found out the tarp had not been put on the field. Hmmmm. Now, I would really like to think that it was an honest mistake, and it truly might have been. Then again, maybe a little gamesmanship was taking place.

We ended up not playing for two more days. By then, their ace was ready to go. To make matters worse, the game was moved to a different field that was just a ten-minute drive from our opponent's school. The beauty of it is that it just didn't matter. My spin on it was that they felt they needed an advantage because they knew we were the better team. I think most coaches and players would have let this get into their heads and affect the outcome of the game. Not us. We thought it was kind of funny. We were going to win anyway and beat their best pitcher along the way. And guess what? We did just that. It was a great ballgame. We played outstanding ball that day. Confidence was exuding from every single one of us the moment we stepped off the bus. Our focus was outstanding that day. We would not be denied.

The New York State Championship

The second incident on the path to our championship involves our ride to the State Final Four site. Our school rented a nice coach bus for us. This was a real treat and a special feeling. It was a brutally hot day. Ninety plus degrees with high humidity.

We had a three-hour drive to our hotel. About forty-five minutes into the trip the air conditioning quit. You have got to be kidding me! We just looked at each other and started to laugh. Perfect. It fits right into the rest of the season. Some mechanical troubles followed, and they had to send another bus to finish the trip. We were late getting to our hotel, missing our practice time on a local field. Once again, this could have been a negative set of circumstances. My take on it was we lucked out. While the other three teams were sweating their butts off and burning up a lot of energy, we were chilling out in our hotel doing a little bonding, and mentally preparing for the next day. What could be better? It was meant to be, and part of the big plan. Thanks for watching over us Tim.

Saturday June 9th was a beautiful day. Perfect weather for the semi-final against Brushton-Moira from section 10. Their school is in the northern tip of New York State a little south of Ottawa and Montreal. This section of the state was known for their elite hockey teams. I mention this because their roster was made up of tough kids who most likely played hockey. They were strong and fast, and not afraid to intimidate their opponents. I distinctly remember their pre-game warmup and how their players were looking into our dugout with body language that suggested we were to be dominated.

The cardinal rule of the state semi-final game is you start your ace on the mound. There is nothing worse than getting sent home with your best pitcher sitting on the bench. I rolled the dice and started my number two pitcher. This was a dangerous move any way you look at it. You think you can have your ace come in and bail him out if he gets into trouble, but what if he gives up three runs and it's too late? My goal was to win the state championship. I had faith in both pitchers, and luckily it worked out for the best.

My number two pitcher, Codi Vanzile, was masterful that day. He gave up one run in the second inning and shut them down until he got into trouble in the fifth inning with two outs, two runners on base and the game tied. It was time to bring in my big gun. Jon Howard struck out the first batter he faced to end the threat. We squeaked out a run in our half of the second inning which gave us the lead.

The way we scored the run in the second inning is the reason I mentioned how tough the kids were from Brushton-Moira. With runners on first and second base and one out, Rob Lindquist turned the tide of the game. Our batter hit a ground ball to short. A sure double play ball which would have ended the inning. Rob took out their second baseman with a hard legal slide knocking the ball loose leaving their second baseman lying flat on the ground.

Their second baseman lay on the ground for several seconds allowing our runner at second Jeremy Sommers to round third and score. That slide sent a message. We would not be intimidated. Our bench was fired up as the momentum shifted in our favor. I was so proud of the tough nosed attitude of our players.

Jon retired seven of the eight batters he faced in relief, with the help of an outstanding diving catch by our center fielder Bryce Cortright. We scored a run on a sacrifice fly in the fifth

The New York State Championship

inning, tacking on three insurance runs in the bottom of the frame. Victory was ours. We finally had the chance to play in a State Championship game.

This was as far as any team in our school history had come. I was excited, but knew there was more work to be done. Winning a State Championship is so elusive. A bounce here, a call there, and you are heading for home without the hardware. As a team, we talked all season long about being on a mission. Our rallying cry was, "Unfinished business." Our lopsided losses in the State Tournament years prior were a thing of the past. I felt confident this time. I was in a good place and focused on the task at hand with clarity and conviction.

We would face Chapel Field from Section 9. Located north of New York City, this team would be another tough test. Luckily for us, while we played Brushton-Moira in the semi-final game, they were playing their semi-final game on a nearby field. Our assistant coach Tony Lewis was able to scout them and pass on some valuable information. More about that later.

There was only a one-hour break between games. Our kids did not celebrate after the semi-final victory. We sat in the shade and ate lunch knowing there was more business at hand. The conversations were muted. This team was all business. One down and one to go. The media had commented several times about our lack of celebration after each playoff win. My answer was simple, we had unfinished business. We would celebrate if we were lucky enough to win a state title as that is our goal. Nothing less would suffice that year.

Our fans filed back into their seats after visiting the concession stand. I could feel their excitement mixed with nervous tension. This was it. The biggest game in school history.

I scanned the stands prior to taking the field for our pre-game warmup. Individual parents were offering encouragement to their sons. "You've got this Kyle, Good luck Rob, We love you guys." Such a big moment.

Naturally, I put our ace Jon Howard back on the mound. He responded by retiring the side in order in the first inning. We loaded the bases with two out in our half of the inning only to have a nice running catch in deep center field end our chance to score. Both pitchers were in top form, putting zeros on the scoreboard for the next two innings.

We scratched out a run in the bottom of the fourth inning when we led off with a ground ball that resulted in two throwing errors and a runner on third base. A pop out to the pitcher for the first out kept our runner at third base. I played a hunch and added one of our second-string players into the lineup as a designated hitter.

Our regular hitter in that slot had been struggling, and I needed someone to put the ball in play. Dylan Ellis, in the biggest at bat of his career, hit a ground ball to the right side bringing the runner home from third base and collecting an RBI in the State title game. We held a 1-0 lead.

Jon continued his dominance but gave up a run in the fifth inning when a lead-off walk and stolen base turned into a run on a throwing error. The game was tied, and you could cut the tension with a knife. You could see it on the faces of the players and fans from both schools. They were hanging on every pitch.

The first inning in a big game is usually a bit sloppy as nerves get the best of the players. It is typical for mistakes to be made early, followed by a period of settling down before the tension rises to a peak as the game is on the line. These last two innings

The New York State Championship

would answer the question of how mentally strong we really were.

One of the biggest plays of the game took place in Chapel Field's top half of the seventh and last inning. Their leadoff batter hit a solid single and promptly stole second base. This is where the scouting report from my assistant coach Tony Lewis came into play. He noted that they loved to fake a bunt in these situations, drawing the third baseman in to field the bunt as the runner on second beat the shortstop to third. It is always a tough play for the shortstop to cover third base in these situations. They had successfully executed this play in their semi-final game.

We discussed this scenario before the game, deciding to keep our third baseman home at the bag and have our pitcher cover the bunt. Sure enough, the batter squared to bunt as the runner at second headed for third. The batter pulled his bat back and our catcher Derek Austin threw a strike to third baseman Rob Lindquist who tagged out the runner. Now the bases were empty with one out and Jon retired the next two batters to keep the game tied.

Jon only faced seven batters over the last two innings as he continued to dominate. However, this would be his last inning as he had reached the limit allowed by New York State pitching regulations. With the game tied, our number nine hitter and catcher Derek Austin stepped to the plate. He hit a soft ground ball to their shortstop beating the throw by a half step. Not willing to take a chance, I played it by the book and gave our leadoff hitter the bunt sign. Unfortunately, he popped out to the pitcher. Good baserunning by Derek allowed him to return safely to first base avoiding a double play.

Chapel Field had replaced their catcher late in the game. It looked like he had injured his throwing arm at some point. If I was ever going to give the steal sign this was it. Touches to the hat, chest and leg let our runner and batter know we were going to steal. The pitch was on the way, our batter faked a bunt, the catcher threw to second base as Derek slid in just under the tag. The table was set.

Our next batter was Kyle Armstrong. He was one of our better hitters; however, he was not having a particularly good tournament at the plate. This was one of those moments that makes baseball such a great game. There is no way to stall or run out the clock. Kyle would get his chance to succeed or fail. He stepped into the batter's box waggling his bat and settling into his stance. The first pitch was a hard fastball right down the middle. Kyle turned on it, hitting a line shot to left center field. Their outfielders had already made several outstanding running catches, but this ball was scorched, and no one was going to catch it. Derek rounded third at a leisurely pace jogging home with me right behind him. He touched home and then, finally; the celebration was on. We were State Champions. It was in the vault and could never be taken away or tarnished. Wow. Tears on the field and in the stands as our loyal fans streamed onto the field. A moment in time that will never be erased.

Our dugout emptied as the entire team converged at home plate. The scene was one of pure joy. Claps on the back, hugs, shouts of joy, and yes, tears. Our fans could not contain themselves. They too were hugging, laughing, and crying. Shouts of "Congratulations," and "You did it, boys," bombarded our senses.

The New York State Championship

I huddled up the team around the mound taking a knee. For a moment I was speechless. I finally blurted out, "Do you realize what you've done? We are State Champions. I'm so proud of you. Take a look into the stands. They are proud of you as well."

The best way to describe how I felt in that moment is surreal. It was such a momentous event for the players, for our school, and for our community that it was hard to comprehend. After chasing the dream for over twenty years was this real? I did take a moment to soak it all in, scanning the stands and field trying to see the entire picture. And what a picture it was.

Parents and friends filtered onto the field for congratulations and pictures. Team pictures, individual shots, our seniors together. So much fun, and so satisfying. The media caught my attention for an interview. I answered all their questions beaming the entire time. Soaking in the rewards of an incredible season.

The bus ride home was one for the books. Storytelling, laughing, and just plain silliness. We stopped along the way to eat, joined by many of the parents. One great big love fest. We boarded the bus for the last leg of the trip home, which led to one of the most emotional moments I have experienced as a coach. As we approached the town of Cherry Creek, which is about two miles from our school, we noticed a large group of people lining the sidewalk.

It was midnight as the bus slowed to a crawl, as we all moved to the passenger side. Each window making it's unique clicking sound as the players squeezed the tabs together and slid them down. The night was still, amplifying the clapping and words of congratulations. For that one moment in time, we were as cool as the night breeze gently blowing on our beaming faces.

We continued our slow roll out of town, heading to our school along a long straight stretch of road. About a half mile from the school one of the players yelled, "Hey coach, you gotta see this." Trailing behind the bus was a long line of cars at least half a mile long. Their headlights perfectly replicated the famous scene from *Field of Dreams*. All I could think of was, "Win it and they shall come." I still get goosebumps whenever I reflect on that night.

I felt a tremendous feeling of accomplishment and satisfaction. Our school district had been in existence for over fifty years. I personally had been chasing the dream of a State Championship for twenty-one years. Bringing home the Holy Grail and seeing the emotions of my players is difficult to put into words. The championship was ours. Forever in the record books. A bond had been created among coach, players, and community that would live on forever.

Once I had time to reflect on what we had accomplished that magical season, I began to piece together the how and the why.

The chapters in this book hold the secrets to our success. Everyone played a role in winning the biggest game of all, as well as winning at the game of life. I encourage you to read each chapter again. Apply every lesson, story, and piece of advice to your life. Do you find comfort in knowing what is truly important? We are not defined by the scoreboard of life. The car we drive, the house we live in, the job we hold, is not the way to keep score. Strive to be a good person. Most importantly, strive to improve the lives of those around you.

In the fourteen years that have passed since that game, I have had the opportunity to talk to most of the players on that team. I have followed their lives as they married and had children. I would like to think I coached for all the right reasons, and had we not won that game we would all still be winners in life.

The trick is to create this mindset within yourself and your team as an intentional thought process rather than as the result of a tragedy. I would not recommend you having to achieve your moment of clarity the way I did. The development of this mindset and the dedication of each coach and player to commit to it and act accordingly, allowing obstacles to become propellers to success, is largely what contributed to the achievement of our ultimate goal.

There is incredible power in the technique of visualization, or the ability to imagine a successful scenario. Just as athletes condition their body, mental imagery provides a way of conditioning the mind for success. Studies show that when athletes visualize a successful skill or competitive outcome, they stimulate the same brain regions as when they physically perform that same action. Incorporating time for visualization and mental imagery exercises into your practices will allow your athletes to envision success, increase positive thought patterns and help players stay confident and focused.

Having that unwavering belief is a wonderful tool to have in your arsenal, but of course you need the skill to go along with it. Confidence also comes from hard work and repetition. This book is not about the fundamentals of the game, but it goes without saying that skill is needed to succeed as well. Confidence is knowing you have worked hard and completed the repetitions necessary to repeat a skill in a game or life situation.

Baseball Is Life Is Baseball

Tim Sercu Senior Year
Photo courtesy of The Post-Journal

The New York State Championship

*NYS Championship Pre-Game Strategy.
Photo courtesy of The Post-Journal*

*More Pre-Game Strategy with Assistant Coach Justin Fish
Photo courtesy of The Post-Journal*

Pre-Game Visualization NYS Championship Game Starting Pitcher Jon Howard
Photo courtesy of The Post-Journal

Jon Howard Dealing
Photo courtesy of The Post-Journal

Jon Howard Celebrating Final Out in the Top of the Seventh Inning
Photo courtesy of The Post-Journal

The New York State Championship

Kyle "Tank" Armstrong. The Shot Heard Round the High School World
Photo courtesy of The Post-Journal

Post-Game Team Huddle
Photo courtesy of The Post-Journal

The New York State Class D Champions
Photo courtesy of The Post-Journal

Championship Rings
Author family photo

New York State Championship #2

I mentioned in one of the first chapters that I was involved in a second NYS Championship. After retiring from teaching at Pine Valley Central school, I was graciously asked by Fredonia Central School head baseball coach Vince Gullo if I would come onboard as an assistant coach. I readily agreed, as I was not ready to retire from coaching entirely. My wife Ann and I moved to Fredonia in 1974 where Ann began her teaching career. This was the village where we raised our children and spent our adult lives.

The Fredonia area had a long tradition of baseball from little league, through high school, as well as the Division III College in town. Many friends and neighbors' children had come up through the system. I was excited to be a part of this rich history.

The year was 2013. My job was to work with the pitchers and catchers. Although my previous coaching experience in a smaller school required me to teach all positions, this was my area of strength. The pre-season consisted of perfecting the mechanics of pitching and catching, along with fielding their positions. The entire package of pick offs, covering first base, bunt defense, throwing out runners, blocking pitches, and all that their positions entailed.

This was a well-established program, having experienced a great deal of success over the years. Living in Fredonia for many years, I was familiar with the program and most of the athletes. This group of athletes were talented, with the potential to have an outstanding season. What jumped out at me was how the mental part of the game needed improvement and could be just the thing to bring out the best in them.

With the approval of head coach Vince Gullo, I began introducing the concepts of playing the game one pitch at a time, controlling what you can control, fear of failure, having fun, visualization, and positive self-talk. I taught them how to recognize when they were losing control of their emotions, and how to get back to the "green light" setting.

As noted earlier in the book, not everyone will buy into what you are selling. This became clear to me at one of the first meetings I had with the team introducing the mental part of the game. The setting was a classroom at the school early in the pre-season. We were still in the indoor part of the Western New York baseball season, which made this the perfect time for some classroom work. Coach Gullo had followed my career at Pine Valley and was aware of our success. He gave me a nice introduction fully onboard with what I was about to teach.

It was immediately apparent that the kids were excited to learn something new. They were highly motivated and looking for any edge that could add to their success. Well, almost all of them were. The head coach left the room to set up the gym for the second half of practice. Once he left, Trent Thompson, arguably the ace of the pitching staff, slid two desks together and promptly laid on top of them with his head down. My teacher mind began analyzing this development. Maybe he had a rough night and was tired. Perhaps, it was to show me that he was good and did not need my help to succeed. I had pretty thick skin and focused my attention on the group that wanted to learn.

When the head coach returned, he admonished the uninterested player who at least sat up and feigned paying

New York State Championship #2

attention. I completed my presentation, moving on with practice as if nothing had happened. I couldn't help thinking about it though. I had watched a couple of games at the end of the previous season, and felt if anyone needed my help, it was Trent. He was a good kid and a talented pitcher, but I noticed the more intense the pressure, the more he committed unforced errors.

Once the season was underway, he began to struggle. The rest of the pitching staff showed improvement while he seemed to digress. I believe it was about halfway through the season he began to talk to the other pitchers about the mental game, eventually approaching me and asking for help.

Fast forward to the New York State semi-finals. The game would take place on Union-Endicott Sylvester Field, a beautiful diamond for such an important game. The weather was perfect with sunny skies, calm wind, and a comfortable temperature. There was a lot of excitement in the air. Like every playoff game leading up to this one, it was win or go home, but to go home one game short of a State Championship would be a harsh blow.

There was a buzz coming from our fans in the stands. They loved baseball and as usual, were out in force to support their team. It was a rare occurrence that another school would have more fans in the stands than we did, and today was no exception. I made it a habit to enjoy the moment. Soaking in the sights and sounds. I scanned the bleachers, recognizing most of the faces. Longtime friends and relations brought together for a common cause. "Good luck coach, you've got this," floated down to me.

The prodigal son was on the mound in the biggest game of his life. Part of my duties was to call pitches. I was prepared for this game like every other playoff game. I had spent a great deal of time scouting our opponents. I voraciously read newspaper clippings, contacted coaches, and scouted live games from behind the plate with my radar gun and clipboard.

Our opponent was Ogdensburg Free Academy. They were ranked #1 in Section 10 having posted a 10-2 league record. Fresh off a 3-1 win in their sectional finals, they were confident and showed it every step of the way. Hitting was one of their strengths and needed our full attention. I felt I knew how to attack them and minimize the damage their potent bats could produce. Was our starting pitcher up to the task?

The kid who took a nap all those days ago in that classroom, threw a complete game six hitter, allowing two unearned runs. He faced two batters over the minimum in the last four innings. We won 9-2 and in just one hour were on our way to a state championship game.

It is difficult, if not impossible, to quantify the effect of the mental training on his performance that day, but I believe it played a role. His body language that day was that of a confident, poised athlete ready for any challenge. He never once waivered from that posture. He was in the moment every step of the way. One pitch at a time over and over again. When the pressure was turned up, he responded and shut it down. I was very proud of him that day. I still am.

The time had come. The State Championship game. We would face the Clinton Warriors from Section 3. This was the last game of the season for both teams. Would we be State Champions or finish second and be relegated to obscurity? Hardly anyone remembers who finished second.

The top of the first inning turned out to be a coach's dream. Clinton's pitcher had been remarkably successful in both league and playoff games that season, but looked nervous to me. We

New York State Championship #2

scored five runs on a leadoff walk followed by six hits and a fielder's choice to plate five runs.

As mentioned earlier, big games like this usually followed a pattern. The first inning is a battle of nerves for both teams. The players settled down after that and played the way they were capable of playing. Once the game gets into the late innings in a close game, everyone tightens up as the magnitude of the situation hits them once again. We had won the battle of the top of the first inning.

Walking out of the dugout and heading to the mound for the bottom of the first inning was sophomore Cam Voss. He was a big lefty with an outstanding fastball and good enough off-speed stuff to keep hitters of balance. He, more than anyone, devoured my teachings on the mental part of the game. He was all in from day one. Today was his final exam.

Cam mowed down Clinton in that first inning, and although he admitted being nervous at first, settled down to pitch the game of his life. Clinton's pitcher settled down as well, allowing only two runs over the last six innings. It didn't matter. Cam Voss took a no hitter into the top of the seventh inning, where he allowed a leadoff single before shutting the door for good.

Clinton coach Tom Pfisterer was quoted as saying of Cam, "He had all the answers. Every time we got ahead in the count, he made the pitch he needed to make, and we did not hit the ball hard off him at all. My hat's off. I understand he's just a sophomore and God bless him; he's going to be a good one."

That quote reinforced everything I had been teaching. Play the game one pitch at a time, control your emotions, nothing matters but the next pitch, no excuses, get on the bump and compete.

Baseball Is Life Is Baseball

The celebration as the fly ball settled into center fielder Nick Hart's glove for the last out was one for the books. The players stormed the mound piling on each other as our fans hugged and cheered, many with tears in their eyes. So many people brought together in this wonderful moment in time by the great game of baseball.

I did not join the on-field celebration. I stood up from my pitch calling perch at the end of the dugout and followed my routine of organizing my charts and notes. This may seem strange to some, but it was my way of finishing a job well done. We put together a plan to complete an objective, executed it to perfection, and this was my routine.

My post game organization routine did not last long. How could it? I greeted the excited players as they returned to the dugout. Sharing hugs and teary-eyed congratulations. The trophy presentation was both rewarding and emotional as parents and fans snapped hundreds of pictures. Once the ceremony ended, we mingled with our many well-wishers receiving congratulations and thanks for making them so proud. I guess bursting with pride is the best way to describe my feelings. I was so proud of what our kids had accomplished, knowing the hard work that led to this moment.

I was also so happy we had brought such joy to so many people. The radio broadcast touched so many people in our community. Fredonia is a small village of hard-working people who support all their local teams with undying passion. They hung on every pitch that day, cheering us on and celebrating our victory.

A job well done, boys. Well-done indeed.

New York State Championship #2

New York State Semi-Final Winning Pitcher Trent Thompson
Photo courtesy of The Post-Journal

*New York State Championship Game Winning Pitcher Cam Voss
Photo courtesy of The Post-Journal*

New York State Championship #2

Fredonia High School Coaches Strategy Session
L-R Tim Cowan, Phil Schrader, Jim Rush, Jake Mc Cune, Charlie LaDuca, Head Coach Vince Gullo, Terry Presto
Photo courtesy of The Post-Journal

New York State Class B Champions. First row far right L-R Trent Thompson and Cam Voss. Notice the Ice Packs
Photo courtesy of The Post-Journal

Personal Wellness

Sport seasons are long and often difficult. They take a mental and physical toll on all involved. It can sneak up on you, and if you are not careful, you will hit a wall. The amount of energy needed to negotiate the numerous situations that arise during a season is incredible. Scheduling, weather delays, discipline issues, transportation, constant communication with athletes, parents, coaches, and administrators, and of course game management. Most coaches have another job. Typically, they are teachers; but in many instances, they have an outside job, which can complicate scheduling of games and practices. They also must balance family commitments.

It took several years before I understood I could not go all out for three months without crashing. I began to take "me" days. I would take a personal day off from teaching, or use a weekend to get away from it all and relax. These days can be used in a variety of ways to clear your mind and rest your body. They are personal to everyone. I played golf, went fishing, took a long bicycle ride, or soaked in a hot tub. Massages are a wonderful idea.

When a full or half day was not possible, I made a point of finding a couple of hours in the evening to relax. A quiet walk or sitting out on the deck watching the sunset usually did the trick. Time to clear my head and think without interruption. Time to put everything into perspective and start the next day refreshed.

I monitored my athletes carefully, assuring that they did not become burned out as well. It's easy to see if you know what to look for. Showing up late when they never have before, changes in demeanor or attitude, just going through the motions at practice. All it takes is a little focus on your part to see it and correct it. I tried my best to have the most rested, sharp team once play-offs rolled around.

This is not only an important skill to acquire for coaches. Life in general, wears everyone down. I would encourage everyone to take "me" days from time to time. Recognize when you have entered the "yellow light" zone and make a correction before it turns to "red." Stress takes a tremendous toll on our minds and bodies. It accumulates slowly, imperceptibly, creeping in and finally taking control.

The best advice I was given on the subject was to take a step back and ask yourself this simple question, "What's the worst that can happen?" Simple, but powerful, if you are honest with yourself. You lost a close game. What's the worst that can happen? You drop a spot in the standings, you do not win your league title, you miss the playoffs? All important things to a coach and your players, but how important? In a world where family and friends are diagnosed with fatal illnesses and tragedy happens every day, was that the worst thing that can happen?

You were still able to teach life lessons making yourself and your players better people. These setbacks are not tragedies. They are teachable moments designed to test you and to make everyone better. They are certainly not the worst thing that can happen. It's all about perspective.

Relate this concept to your everyday life. What has stressed you out in the past? A flat tire or traffic jam? Your favorite team lost a football game? A minor car accident? Travel plans interrupted by things out of your control? I could add more serious things to the list, but, in retrospect, how serious? Take a deep breath and ask yourself, "What's the worst that can happen?"

Baseball Is Life Is Baseball

Baseball has shaped my life in ways I never thought possible. A simple, yet not so simple game, has played an integral role in who I am today. My father Sam instilled the values and character qualities in me that made me a successful player and coach. Rising early in the morning and returning late at night, he led by example. Dad was a truck driver, earning a modest living for my mom and three siblings. He was a hard worker with a strong moral compass, at ease around people from all walks of life. Whether you were a doctor, lawyer, factory worker, or janitor, Sam LaDuca found a way to find common ground and, at some point, make you laugh. His natural ability to be at ease and to find humor in most situations made him popular in many social circles.

The lessons I learned from my father fit perfectly with success on the field. Work hard, have fun, strive to be the best, exhibit good character, learn from your mistakes, never fear failure, have strong discipline, and treat people the way you would like to be treated. Applying these character qualities to my baseball and coaching career translated into success, but also carried over to my life off the field. My on-field success reinforced the importance of the lessons I learned growing up and became a template for my life off the field.

The story I am about to tell perfectly illustrates the title of this book. There have been many emotional moments in my sixty-two years of playing and coaching, none more emotional than the events that took place in the fall of 2003.

My first trip to the Men's Senior Baseball League World Series was in October of 1994. I pitched against a team from Boston at Doubleday Field earlier that summer and had a good outing. The manager of the opposing team asked me to join him in Arizona for the World Series. I was teaching at the time, and not sure I could get the time off. The first order of business was to convince my wife Ann that this was a once in a lifetime chance to compete at a high level.

I took Ann out to dinner and pleaded my case. Being the good baseball wife that she was, she agreed. Next up was getting my school to give me the time off to attend. I taught in a small rural school with outstanding administrators. They thought it was an honor and found a way for me to use my personal days to make the trip. They even put together a little farewell ceremony involving my elementary students. I was made to feel like a celebrity, a feeling I will never forget. I wish I had recorded the speech I gave my wife regarding the 'once in a lifetime trip,' because twenty-eight years later I am still competing in the Men's Senior Baseball League World Series.

The story begins with my second trip to the World Series in the fall of 1994. I invited my father and father in-law to join me. They eagerly agreed, and off we went.

The games were played on numerous spring training sites in Phoenix and the surrounding areas. Beautiful stadiums, blue skies, and that comforting dry heat that loosens the muscles and guarantees you will play every day. Add a sprinkling of former Major League players in the mix and we were all in baseball heaven.

Sharing a hotel room, and having breakfast and dinner with my dad and father in-law that week was the *true* once in a lifetime experience. We talked about baseball, family, golf, and all the things three good friends would discuss on such a trip. One conversation flowed into the next. Easy, casual conversation filled with laughter and stories of the good old days. A moment in time made possible by the great game of baseball.

Sam and Red came to every game, soaking in the sights and sounds while serving as official video recorders of the trip. On an off day we took a trip to Sedona, Arizona to see the sights and play a round of golf. The scenery was spectacular, surpassed only by the bonding that took place. Later in the week we snuck another round of golf in as our trip came to an end. My dad and father in-law reminisced about our trip from that day forward until the day they died.

The following year my father in-law was not able to make the trip, but my dad did. It was another memorable trip with baseball, food, golf, and sunshine blending together to create magic that is so hard to find. Fast forward to 2003 when baseball and life collided to break my heart.

I was teaching elementary physical education in 2003 and had just finished a swimming class when my phone rang. It was my mother, and she was sobbing uncontrollably. My father had been diagnosed with stage four lung cancer and been given six months to live. Those few halting words, spoken amid heart wrenching sobs, completely devastated me. My best friend, the man who meant the most to me, was just sentenced to a slow horrible death.

My father smoked three packs of cigarettes a day since he was a teen. We made several attempts to get him to quit without success. One morning he woke up at two o'clock, opened a fresh pack of Lucky Strikes and had a smoke. Later that morning he picked up his assignment for his truck route that day, reached for a cigarette, and saw there was only one left. He crumbled the pack, threw it in the trash, and never touched a cigarette again. That was thirty years before I received the call that changed my life.

I lived an hour drive from my parents' home. This is the same house that I grew up in. My wife Ann and our daughters Laura and Lindsey visited frequently, but in retrospect, not frequently enough. Dad developed a cough that lingered for a few weeks, but in western New York coughs and the sniffles were common. He was a tough guy and wrote it off to seasonal allergies or a cold. I don't know what finally made him visit a doctor, but I do know that it was too late.

The next months were a steady decline in dad's health. Cancer is cruel and I hate it with all my heart. My father refused to give in. He got up every morning, took a shower, shaved, and tried to have a decent day. My visits were incredibly difficult. It tore me up to see what was happening to the strong, humorous man I had known my entire life. To this day I regret not visiting more than I did. It hurt to see him that way. It was selfish on my part. I could not stand to see him suffer, and my weakness denied him time with his oldest son.

The following months were a blur of visits to the oncologist, family gatherings, long conversations, and a pretense that all was normal, but the die was cast. The clock was ticking, and my father did not have long to live.

I was scheduled to play in the Men's Senior Baseball League's World Series that October. I had started a small wood bat company the year before and would be doing double duty as a vendor at the trade show and as a ball player. Flights, rental car, trade show booth, and hotel had all been booked months in advance. This was a big commitment, but not bigger than my father's needs.

I paid a visit to my dad to see how he was doing, trying to decide on the best course of action. Selfishly, once again, I was trying to play ball while being there for my father as well.

It is hard for me to admit that baseball was even a consideration at that point, but that is the power baseball had over me, and still does. We had a long talk, and I was assured he was fine and would see me when I returned a week later. Honestly, there was nothing that led me to believe this would not be the case. I was wrong.

I arrived in Phoenix on a Saturday, picked up my rental car, checked into the hotel, and headed off to practice. The next few days were divided between playing and selling bats at the trade show. A grueling schedule that left me exhausted. I called my dad every day to update him on my progress. He seemed upbeat as we talked about the details of the games, the weather, bat sales and of course his health. Throughout his entire ordeal, he never wanted anyone to feel sorry for him. He did his best every day to act and think as if all was well. An admirable trait for someone going through a living hell.

We played a doubleheader on Wednesday. After the game, I called my dad from the parking lot, and something was off. The minute he started talking a feeling rushed over me that something was not right. It was subtle, but I could sense that he was losing the battle. We hung up and I cried like a baby. I tried to recover before my teammates joined me, but simply could not. My eyes were red, and I was obviously distraught.

This was the beginning of my baseball family showing their love for a teammate. They consoled me doing their best to help in any way they could. Although I had a relatively stress-free life as a child, the ball field was always a place to forget everything but baseball for a couple of hours. It had worked my entire life. This was different. Now, you would think I would have immediately tried to book a flight for home. Once again, I convinced myself that my dad would be okay until I returned. He would want me to keep playing. Two incredible life forces were pulling at me-baseball and my father. It should have been an easy decision.

I played again Thursday and called my dad after the game. He seemed better than the day before. Only three more days to go. Friday was a late game. I worked my booth in the morning and played late that afternoon. I had just finished my game and gone back to the trade show booth when my phone rang. It was my wife and her voice told me I had run out of time. She said my father had gone downhill very quickly. I asked her to put me on the phone. She told me that he probably could not hear me but put the phone to his ear. I talked to him like all was well. I told him about the game and how much I loved him. My wife told me later that although he was in a coma, he smiled.

The race was on to drop everything and get home as fast as I could. I cannot thank my teammates, and the MSBL's staff and administrators for their herculean effort to get me home. I had to find a red-eye flight, pack my bats and bags, and get to the airport. The baseball family that I had been accumulating for over ten years dropped everything and made my welfare a priority. They made it happen, wishing me well and offering prayers as I headed to my gate.

I arrived at my parent's house at five o'clock Saturday evening. My father was in bed surrounded by my mother, brothers, sister, and my wife. He looked frail, eyes closed, taking rapid shallow breaths. We hugged and cried as we watched the life slowly leave the man we loved so much. At some point I laid down on the couch in the living room exhausted. I was gently awakened by my brother at three o'clock in the morning telling me he thought the time had come. We gathered at the bedside as my father's breathing began to slow. In and out, in and out, slower and slower until it stopped. There was a five second pause, one last breath and he was gone.

Heads hung low, we cried consoling each other. My mother asked for some time alone with my father. She climbed into bed and laid beside him one last time as we left the bedroom. We contacted the police and funeral director as my mother came from the bedroom gently closing the door.

Two policemen arrived first. They were exceedingly kind, offering condolences in an awkward sort of way. Within minutes the funeral director and his assistant arrived. We waited in the living room as they performed their duties, eventually emerging from the bedroom with my father on a stretcher. He looked so small. It was far too easy for them to carry him. I followed them to their vehicle walking like a zombie in a trance trying to say a final goodbye. The night was so still and quiet. The sound of the van doors closing jolted me back to reality. Life was different now.

It was difficult for me to put this on paper. Typing was frequently interrupted by tears and memories. I leave it to the reader to take whatever they will from this chapter. For me, it illustrates the power of sport as it relates to life. They are intertwined in so many ways. Lessons are always flowing back and forth between the two. Baseball like life, has given me many blessings, and I am forever grateful.

The Three Amigos
L-R Charlie LaDuca, Sam LaDuca, Red Walsh
Author family photo

Sam LaDuca Video Camera at the Ready
Author family photo

Sam and Charlie LaDuca
Bell Rock Sedona, Arizona
1994 MSBL World Series
Author family photo

Sport Imitates Life

Once I sat down and began to write this book, I realized it was as much about successful life skills as it was about baseball skills. The mental skills and strategies I used on the field were also critical to success off the field.

When I think about the chapters in this book: Confidence, Motivation, Fear of Failure, Discipline, Dress for Success, Control What You Can Control, Communication, Team Building, and Coaching for Character, it is easy to see that this is also a recipe for success off the field.

One of the jobs I had before I began my teaching and coaching career was that of a store manager for Montgomery Ward. Now there is a blast from the past. Our Regional Manager was a rising star in the organization. His name was George Wallace. He was only thirty-two-years-old at the time. He made it a point to hire athletes as his store managers. It was a brilliant strategy. The retail business is extremely competitive, and we were only as good as the previous week's sales. Every week he would put us all on a conference call to review our sales numbers. He played us against each other week after week. Our competitive nature took over, and we made him a super star. He realized that our athletic background was a perfect fit for the job at hand.

After reading this book, take a few moments to think about life situations and how to apply these lessons in your daily life. How many strategies can you incorporate into your daily life? Could you reduce stress? Become a better communicator? Learn to analyze your successes and mistakes? Would it be possible to eliminate the fear of failure? Maybe, most importantly, could you play the game of life one day at a time with joy in your heart?

The Final Inning

All things must pass, and so it is with my playing career. The partial knee replacements that have allowed me to play baseball for these past sixteen years have finally worn out. I made an appointment with the surgeon who performed the original operation, hoping beyond hope, the pain I was feeling could be managed somehow. Did I have more time to enjoy the game I loved so much?

The x-rays revealed artificial parts worse for wear. The bone beneath the parts was deteriorated and fragile. I needed two full replacements if I were to walk normally and be pain free. A bitter pill to swallow, yet not a surprising one. Although I can pitch effectively at a very high level in senior tournaments, I'm unable to run at more than a painful jog. The pride I took in playing the game all out, with speed in the outfield, and headfirst slides on the bases, was long gone. A groundball with a runner on first was now an automatic double play. I could no longer play the outfield, relegated to first base, sharing time with four other senior players in the same boat.

Other than pitching, I had become "that guy." The time has come to end my career. I had been working diligently in preparation for the three tournaments I planned on attending as part of the MSBL World Series in Phoenix, Arizona. This would be my twenty-ninth and final appearance, followed by two Roy Hobbs tournaments in February in Fort Myers, Florida.

The question was, would I bow out gracefully, or crash and burn leaving a sour taste in my mouth? What did the baseball gods have in store for me?

I consider myself an ambassador for the game of baseball. I try to play the game the way it was meant to be played. Compete hard, display sportsmanship, and respect my opponents. I continue to work with young players, teaching them the fundamentals of the game, while being positive and encouraging every step of the way. Had I earned enough good karma to be smiled upon in the end? I'm not sure my good deeds made a difference, but I am sure it turned out to be the best two weeks of my life on a ball field.

The first tournament was the 70+ National Division with the LA Athletics. We had a twenty-nine man roster, and by all accounts, were the team to beat. My role that week was in relief along with a couple of at bats here and there. I had worked hard in the three months leading up to the tournament. Weekly bullpen sessions with long toss, heavy ball work, and trips to the gym. It took a toll on my knees, but my arm felt strong.

There is not an age-appropriate league locally, meaning I do not play competitively. My summers are filled with working out and preparing for five tournaments each year. I mention this because typically the first two innings I pitch live in Arizona are a bit shaky.

This year was no exception. Although I never got into trouble, it was not until halfway through the second inning that I settled down regaining my command. I was where I wanted to be, inducing pop ups, lazy fly balls, and double play ground balls. I

The Final Inning

was not going to throw the ball by anybody. My goal was to keep the hitters off balance, not allowing them to drive the ball.

We went 5-1 in pool play. Miraculously, I felt comfortable with all my pitches. Each outing got better than the previous one. My twelve to six curveball was the best it had been in years. Manager Bob Sherwin had assembled an all-star team of great players and even better teammates. We all had one goal. Get that ring. With every player doing their part, we won the championship game with a dominating 10-2 performance. I love the feeling once the last out is recorded and you get to hoist the trophy. It's true, winning never gets old. This win however was bittersweet. I knew several players on the opposing team, and knew that they were disappointed. The Sacramento 70's was an excellent team. They played the game the right way battling hard until the end.

The first tournament and Championship was in the books. On to the 65+ National Division which started the very next day. A tournament, that after all my years of competing, would bring an unexpected emotional surprise.

A quiet victory celebration was followed by dinner and then off to bed. Several of us were staying in a rented house in Scottsdale.

My phone rang at midnight waking me from a sound sleep. It was my wife Ann. My first thought was that my ninety-nine-year-old mother had taken ill. Ann asked what I was doing. I reminded her of the three-hour time difference, telling her I had been sleeping. "Why don't you come outside," she said. A strange request as she was back home in New York and it was midnight. She is not a drinker, but my second thought was that she had gotten a little tipsy and wanted to look at the moon together to do a little bonding.

I walked out the door and there she was with my two daughters, Laura and Lindsey. I was stunned. Ann had only accompanied me to Arizona once in all my years of playing. My daughters had only heard stories once I returned, yet here they were. They knew that my playing days were coming to an end and they wanted to see what this was all about for themselves.

We hugged and kissed, and yes, I did get a bit emotional. They had been planning this for several weeks. I had no idea. We talked for a while, and they returned to their nearby hotel. They were only in town for the weekend. The next morning, I contacted our manager Bob Sherwin and asked for a favor. Although I was not scheduled to pitch that day, could I get on the mound for an inning or two? Being the outstanding person that he is, Bob agreed.

I threw four innings of relief getting the win. Whoever oversees baseball magic gave me my best stuff of the tournament. With my family sitting behind the plate I threw four shutout innings with only three balls leaving the infield. This was one of the highlights of my career. The next day we had a late afternoon game. A perfect time to take a morning trip to Sedona, which is one of my favorite stops when I'm in Phoenix. Sharing the beauty and majesty with them was special indeed.

Later that day was a stadium game under the lights. Although I did not play, Ann and the girls enamored themselves to the team with their exuberant cheering. We won the game in solid fashion, as we began our quest for another championship. They had an early flight, so we said our goodbyes after the game. I must admit, there was a lump in my throat as they drove away.

The Final Inning

Once again, the game of baseball offered the opportunity to make special memories to last a lifetime.

This Division was loaded with excellent teams. We might be considered favorites based on past success, but this year was different. We had a target on our back, and teams were saving their best for us as the tournament progressed. Once again, my role was to pitch in relief. My job was to keep the score where it was and put out fires. I did my job picking up a save in a strange way.

With a 12-4 led in the last inning, a couple of our relievers entered the game and struggled. Eventually, the score was 12-10 with runners on first and second. I quickly warmed up and was given the nod. A high-pressure situation for sure, but I felt confident. I was able to induce a game ending groundball double play. Mission accomplished.

We went undefeated in pool play with a 6-0 record, but it was not easy. Every man on the roster was at his best that week, with solid pitching, stellar defense, and timely hitting. A recipe for success at any level. The stage was set. We would face the Sacramento Tribe. This is the team we defeated 12-10 in pool play when I got the save. It was also comprised of several players from the 70's team who we had defeated in the championship game. Both teams had saved their ace pitcher for this battle.

The game turned out to be a classic pitchers' duel. Both hurlers putting zeroes on the scoreboard inning after inning. Their pitcher doing an outstanding job of keeping our potent offense off balance, with ours doing the same. We scored first with a solo run, and they responded with one of their own. The game sat at 1-1 for several innings before we tacked on a run with a small miscue by the Tribe and some alert baserunning on our part. We now entered the part of the game where both teams held their breath with every pitch thrown.

Our ace, Mike Denevi, had been magnificent for the entire game. He had a partial knee replacement six months prior to the start of the tournament. It was obvious he was running out of gas, but he is one tough guy. Dancing in and out of trouble, he managed to record the final out and the ring was ours. A hard fought 2-1 victory.

We lined up for the traditional handshake, expressing mutual admiration with each shake, fist bump, or high five. Two teams playing the game they were so passionate about, accepting the outcome as gentlemen. We strode to the parking lot side by side. Warriors discussing the battle, wishing each other good luck, and safe travels home. A sigh of relief, and on to the Father/Son Tournament.

The Father/Son Tournament is a wonderful format. Fathers get a chance to play with their sons, nephews, stepsons, and son-in-laws. Daughters are eligible to play as well. Four fathers must be in the field at all times and sons may not bat back-to-back in the batting order more than twice. I did not have a son playing with nephews or a son-in-law over the years.

We have played in several divisions over the years predicated by the college experience of the sons on our roster. The last several years have placed us in the tough Federal Division. Our sons are excellent players, but our fathers are up in age.

Although we are all decent players, truth be told, we hold the team back. We had never made it to a championship game prior to this year.

This year our top three son pitchers were not able to make the trip. We did pick up one excellent son pitcher, but were not as

The Final Inning

strong at that position compared to years past. Our Federal Division would be combined with the upper National Division for pool play. All seven teams would make the playoffs, with the top four competing for the National title and the bottom three for the Federal title. The interesting twist was that the number five seed would draw a bye to the Federal Division Championship game.

Once again, the magic continued. When pool play finished, we were tied with a team we had not played. The first tie breaker was runs against. Both teams sat at thirty-three. The next tie breaker was runs scored and we would lose in that category. We thought we were the number six seed and must play our way into the championship game. Hold on a second. We noticed one of our scores had been incorrectly recorded. A 3-1 loss was recorded as 4-1. The correction was made, and we were now the number five seed. Think about all the action taking place in our four pool play games. Giving up just one more run would have made us the six seed. We started to believe we were a team of destiny.

The game was scheduled for two o'clock at Tempe Diablo Stadium. Another beautiful day. Comfortable temperature in the mid-eighties, with a clear blue sky and just a hint of a breeze. Our opponent was the 3n2 Rangers. A good team with some strong pitching from their sons. We decided to mix things up and start with our best son pitcher on the mound rather than the traditional father toeing the slab. We felt Joe could hold them down giving us a chance to perhaps have a lead after his four innings of work. The strategy worked, and then some. He faced one batter over the minimum in his four innings of work allowing one hit with five strikeouts and no walks.

We scored two runs in the first inning, which is where the score remained until the two fathers came in to pitch in the fifth

L-R daughter Laura, wife Ann, Charlie, daughter Lindsey
Author family photo

The Final Inning

65+ National division champions, Athletics Lonestars BBC, defeated the Sacramento Solons 2-1 in an incredibly competitive game. The Athletics finished the tournament undefeated

Front row: L-R - Don Bixby, Blaine Olson, Dan Coleman, Dave Dietrich, Charlie LaDuca, Mike Thatcher, Bob Sherwin, Dave Howard, Joel Morley, Mike Barraza, Dan Little. Back row: left to right - Craig Aramaki, Hector Gonzalez, Gino Suter, Ron Piacenti, Joe Williamson, Artie Collazo, Mike Denevi, Les Reill, Bill Brown, Bill Mitchell, Doug Springford, Paul McPherson, John Arnold, Mike Patrick, Terry Teske
Author family photo

2021 Father/Son Federal Division National Champions
L-R front row: Tom Roberts, Tyler Roberts, Pete Lacongo, Charlie LaDuca, Ralph Proulx, Tilo Mendiola, Alex Dusenberry, Joe Crisci II, Nick Barberio. L-R back row: Steve Pantano, Brent Carmello, Allan Carmello, Dennis Gawronski, Pat Ruggerio Sr., Ricky Mendiola, Sean Mahoney, Ryan Balbierz, Dave Balbierz, Pat Ruggerio Jr., Joe Crisci III, John Barberio, Tommy LaCongo
Author family photo

Acknowledgements

To my father Sam who led by example. Without knowing the vernacular, he taught a class in character education every day. He was a hard-working truck driver who somehow found time to play catch and throw batting practice often with one baseball covered in electrical tape. He took me to minor league baseball games in Buffalo where we sat through doubleheaders eating peanuts and soaking in the sights and sounds of the great game of baseball. The older I get, the more I realize how much we were alike. I inherited his sense of humor along with many of his mannerisms and sayings. Those terrible "dad jokes" are now passed on to my grandchildren which elicits the same groaning response I gave my dad. I received many gifts from my father, but the greatest of all was his love of baseball. It has shaped much of my adult life, and for that I am eternally grateful. I miss him every day.

To my mother who ruled our house with love and firm discipline. I would not be where I am today without her guidance and unwavering love. Mom is ninety-nine-years-old and living independently. She is sharp as ever, driving all over town to the supermarket, to church, or to the "old folk's" home to help out. An inspiration to all.

To my daughters Laura and Lindsey who have suffered through my many absences as I coached or played ball. It seemed every time they were injured, I was at a game, or at a coaching clinic. They are bright and articulate following in our path as educators. We live two miles apart and have the opportunity to

Acknowledgements

see them and our three grandchildren as often as we like. This is a true blessing.

My sons-in-laws AJ and Kyle bring so much joy. We share many interests including golf and baseball. They have both played with me in our local baseball league with AJ joining me in Arizona one year.

To my fellow coaches, teammates, and players who have provided me with a lifetime of memories. Sharing the field with them has provided me with a life that can only be described as a fairy tale.

To my wife Ann who has somehow stayed by my side for forty-eight years tolerating my obsession with baseball. She cringes as I limp around the house after a game concerned about my welfare. Although it hurts her to see me this way, she understands my passion for the game and has supported me throughout this seemingly never-ending journey. A great teammate.

To Frank Amoroso who has inspired me on and off the field. A fellow lefty pitcher who has written ten books and has guided me through this labor of love. He has brought out the best in me.

References

Langens, Thomas. (2002). *Tantalizing Fantasies: Positive Imagery Induces Negative Mood in Individuals High in Fear of Failure.* Imagination, Cognition and Personality. 21. 281-292.

Manning, Zachary (2017). *Do Participation Trophies Hurt Our Motivation? Some Say Yes.* Spartan News Room. March 21, 2017.

Kleingeld, A., van Mierlo, H., & Arends, L. (2011). "The effect of goal setting on group performance: A meta-analysis." *Journal of Applied Psychology,* 96(6), 1289-1304.

Locke, E. A., & Latham, G. P. (2006). "New Directions in Goal-Setting Theory." *Current Directions in Psychological Science,* 15(5), 265-268.

Blewett, Dan. *Elite Baseball Performance*

Jaeger, Alan. "Getting Focused Staying Focused"

Kuehl, Karl. *The Mental Game of Baseball*

Ravizza, Ken and Hanson, Tom. *Heads Up Baseball*

Vernacchia, Ralph, McGuire, Rick, Cook, David. *Coaching Mental Excellence*

Cain, Brian. *Pitching The Mental Game*

McCown, Lowrie. "Coaching for Life"

Arterburn, Stephen "Winning at Work without Losing at Home"

Bickle, Bruce. "Live Bold and Bloom, List of Good Character Traits Essential for Happiness"

www.ingramcontent.com/pod-product-compliance
Lightning Source LLC
LaVergne TN
LVHW051600070426
835507LV00021B/2692